Child Training and the Home School

A Legacy of Grace

by Jeff and Marge Barth

Parable Publishing House

© 1991 by Jeff Barth
ISBN 0-9624067-2-4

CONTENTS

	Page
Introduction	1

Chapter

1	Facing the Facts	3
2	The Place of Authority	11
3	How Parents Have Lost the Authority	17
4	Taking the Authority	29
5	Gaining Control Through One Requirement	39
6	Understanding Willfulness	47
7	The Beauty of a Subjective Will	53
8	Three Major Areas of Child Behavior Influence	59
9	Legality and Grace in Child Training	65
10	The Rod Gives Wisdom	71
11	The Grace Phase in Child Training	81
12	Family Bonding	97
13	Ministering to the Spirit of Your Child	107
14	Further Spiritual Training	123
15	Character and Social Lifestyle	139
16	Home Schooling, A Road To Greater Success	155

Child Training and the Home School
A Legacy of Grace

INTRODUCTION

One Sunday as my wife, our five young children, and I were leaving a church that we had visited that morning, we were stopped by a mother with her two young children whom I had noticed had sat behind us during the service.

While gazing from one of our children to another, she blurted out, "How do you do it, I mean, train your children?! I was watching them, and I've never seen children act so well." I didn't quite know how to answer her, and before I could, she continued, "I don't believe as Christians we should have to learn everything by our own experience. Could you tell me what you do in your child training?"

This was not the first time we had been complimented in this way by people who had observed our family in restaurants and other public places. I remember one time talking with a friend of mine who was the owner of a nice home furnishings store. When we all walked into his store one afternoon, he immediately put his staff on "red alert" when he saw our five young children. At first he thought his place was at the mercy of five unpredictable kids who, if they were anything like most others their age, would shortly leave his store in ruins.

Within moments, he and his staff stood smiling in astonishment as they observed our polite, calm, and loving children. We were there for nearly an hour, and as I was making payment to my friend while my wife and children were in the other room, he asked me quietly in amazement, "What did you threaten your kids with to make them behave so well in here?!"

I laughed and explained that they usually acted that way—

not that our children were any different—neither were they so-called "good kids"—but that we as parents had learned that if we made the effort and took the time to instill in them proper conduct at home, then they could be expected to act that way in public.

Another time I was in a store with my family buying a wood stove. The proprietor complimented my wife and me on our respectful and obedient children; however, we were used to getting such compliments, so I politely thanked him and let it be at that. But the impression was so strong on the man that the next day when I returned to pick up the stove, he said to me, "Mr. Barth, I want you to know I was serious yesterday when I said that about your children. I'm a former school teacher, and I have never seen children behave so well."

At this point, feeling that God may have been using the situation, I explained that we tried to live and train our children by Biblical principles, and to those Scriptures and God's grace we owed our success. He seemed somewhat surprised; and as our conversation continued, I was able to present the gospel to him, which he received warmly.

Successful, Biblical child training not only brings reward and satisfaction to the parents and children, but also demonstrates to the world around us the truth of the Holy Scriptures and the reality that Christianity can offer the family a better way of life.

There are millions of people today who would like to see such examples. The Christian community can demonstrate this, provided that Christian parents are willing to make their family life their first priority in Christian service and are willing to take the steps to live differently than the world around them.

1

FACING THE FACTS
-Evil Communications Corrupt Good Manners-

"Do not be so deceived and misled! Evil companionships (communion, associations) corrupt and deprave good manners and morals and character." I Corinthians 5:33 Amplified Bible

Evil communications is by far one of the most significant causes of childhood behavioral problems, but it is a cause which usually goes overlooked. Many parents today are misled, as this Scripture suggests, into thinking that wrong associations (communications and companions) will have little impact on their child's behavior.

Our oldest son came to Christ at a young age, as did all our children, and many other home schooling parents have also had the joy of leading their young children to Christ. We contribute this success mostly to our home training environment; and in each of our children, upon coming to Christ, we have observed God's presence in their lives motivating them to righteous living, faith, love for one another, and a love for God and His Word.

These qualities were particularly strong in our oldest son. He was the kind of child that mothers wish their children could be like—compliant, cheerful, agreeable, compassionate, and loving. But then it was time to begin school.

I checked into Christian schools and sent him to what was considered by most of our Christian friends to be the best Christian school around. After only a few, short weeks of school, my wife and I began to observe discouraging changes in our son's personality and spirit. He no longer wanted to trust God for every little thing and to encourage me to do so. Prayer and faith had become less important to him, he for the first time was showing aggression and jealousy toward his younger brother, and his openness with me had grown a little silent. "What was happening?" I wondered.

My son and I were very close, and for the first week or two of school he talked freely on our thirty minute drive to and from school, but now he had become quieter. At first, I just tried to reason it away as a part of growing up, but I did worry somewhat as to what I would face when the teen-age years approached if I was having trouble already keeping communication lines open.

About this same time, a so to speak "nice" Christian lady offered to take my son to school with her car pool and save me the inconvenience and expense of driving back and forth every day. I declined the offer having never felt that time spent with my children was an inconvenience but rather a privilege since I considered my family as my first work for Christ.

I could sense that these attitudes my son was acquiring were the product of his associations (socialization) at school. I knew he was facing temptations from certain classmates (I was able to pry that much out of him), so in an effort to strengthen him, I suggested we try learning Bible verses together as we drove to school. We kept this practice up for some time, but this did little to improve things. I was beginning to feel the examples he was observing at school were too strong an influence upon him.

I knew personally many of the teachers in the school, and they, for the most part, were sincere Christians and kept fairly firm discipline. Why was my son thus having these struggles?

The first school year finally passed, and after a few short weeks into summer vacation, my son, to our relief, began to return to his old self again. He wanted to pray that the Lord would start that old lawn mower I used to get so frustrated with. He looked forward to taking that walk with me at dusk to watch the sunset across the back of the cornfield and to have a time of prayer with me. His compassionate, gentle spirit returned as he once again opened up himself to his mother and me, and his jealousy towards his younger brother disappeared.

However, when school resumed in the fall and after only a few short weeks into the new school year, we began again to be disheartened with our son's attitude. At first we didn't want to place the blame on the school. We had already gotten rid of our TV and many of the children's books which seemed so innocent but subtly promoted aggression, foolishness, pride, disrespectful talk, independence, etc.

We had also become much more selective with the friends and acquaintances we wanted influencing our children. But the one thing that we were beginning to realize was that we had little control of our son's environment at school where he spent most of his time.

I was a young Christian, but I already recognized that many well-meaning Christians could be very worldly and also have misbehaving children. I had no control over the reading materials that passed through my son's hands and mind, and I certainly had none over his classmates and the influences they would have on him daily; but we thought it was that particular school, so we tried several other Christian church schools only to meet with the same results.

Again with the return of summer vacation, the struggles of the past school year were shortly left behind. This cycle went on for three years before God finally brought along a very effective solution to this problem...the home school.

That was many years ago. We are at the time of this writing into our thirteenth year of home schooling, and years have passed since my oldest son first attended those Christian schools. Since then, we have had opportunities to meet many home schooling families and have found that frequently this was the same experience they had with their children when placed in a group school situation.

Gregg Harris of Christian Life Workshops, a seminar for home schooling, made a similar observation with his son.

When our son, Joshua, was five years old, my wife and I thought that since he was an only child, he needed more social interaction. So we sent him to preschool three days a week at a nice Christian school. It was just half a day each time. Over a six-week period, however, we watched our son's personality change dramatically, and we didn't know why.[1]

Dr. Raymond Moore in his many years of experience with home schooling expresses the same problem this way:

The young child learns by observation and imitation. He learns all the time, whether we plan to teach him or not. When he is put with a group of little children he imitates them. He has no way of sorting out the bad from the good. As a matter of fact, we know that he learns the bad more easily than the good. And in general little children are clearly not models of good social and moral values. They are naturally self-centered. They have not yet developed much of a conscience. They adapt quickly to bad habits, manners, language, and morals.[2]

The Apostle Paul warns us of the dangers of these negative, social contacts and cautions us that these influences can be overlooked. "Do not be so deceived and misled! Evil companionships (communion, associations) corrupt and deprave good manners and morals and character." I Corinthians 15:33 Amplified Bible

Of course, this admonition was written mostly to adult Christians as a word of caution; how much more then would it apply to children who haven't passed through a period of Christian training which would establish them in a pattern of righteous living?

But the point is this—that bad corrupts the good and not vice versa. The good doesn't rub off on the bad. If someone suggests that their mischievous child plays with your proper child so that theirs can learn from yours, do not be misled, for you will soon have to be dealing with behavior problems in your own child.

It isn't uncommon for an older child who has been sent away to preschool or school to pick up some wrong behavior habits such as teasing, arrogance, aggression, or excitability and then bring these home and pass them on to one of his or her siblings. This child not only has the support of those at school for these negative ways, but now has a brother or sister at home to further encourage them; and poor mother has a double battle on her hands. How much easier it would have been to have prevented this from ever starting.

The school room is certainly not the only source of "evil communication" in life, but it probably does the most damage because that is where a child spends the most time during the years when they are most vulnerable; and daily contact with negative behavior soon makes a child feel this behavior is acceptable and commonplace. The child may even think that the parents are unreasonable if they challenge some of this behavior that he or she brings home, because after all, they have the support of a classroom of kids, many of whom act the same way, and probably also one or two adults who haven't voiced any opposition to this behavior.

This child is in a very difficult situation where if he is to keep peace and be accepted at school and at home, he must learn to live a double standard and may very likely develop a dual personality. This child may learn to put on a "show" of righteousness at home; and upon reaching adolescence where peer pressure becomes too strong, this young person yields and begins acting out in ways which seem very surprising to the parents. For years, the parents assumed that everything was going fine with their child—and now wonder, "What happened?!"

Most Christian psychologists insist that teen-age conflicts are not only certain but normal, and, of course, their statistics are based on information gathered from parents who have allowed their children to be raised in a group schooling environment or who are regularly involved in teen group associations. But many home schooling parents have discovered as we have that there needn't be the so-called "troublesome teen years" in child training if they have carefully maintained and guided the younger years.

Parents must begin when their children are young scrutinizing every source of evil communication. Most parents of toddlers know how important it is to scrupulously rid the bottom of their cabinets of any household cleaners or poisons which could harm their child, but many well-meaning parents just blindly allow their children to be subjected to sources of behavioral poisons.

Some Other Examples of Evil Communications

Just taking a child out of school is a big help, but it isn't enough. We, as parents, can very easily bring into our own homes varied sources of evil communication.

Carefully and wisely consider the stories you read to your youngster. If there is aggression present whether in the good character or the bad, you will be putting wrong ideas into your child's mind. Are there situations in the story or illustrations which would seem very fearful to your child? This can produce insecurities and a lack of faith that God is in control. Some stories make independence (the first step towards rebellion) look fruitful and exciting.

There are many other negatives being presented in children's literature like pride, deceit, sarcasm, disrespect, hatred, teasing, independence, emphasis on outward or physical beauty, aggression, excitedness, etc. Many of these negative qualities are presented through the means of cartoons and other similar programming.

Minimize your exposure to TV and very closely monitor it—or better yet, don't have one at all. We got rid of our TV when our children were very young and have never regretted it. My wife and I were raised on TV and are periodically tempted with it, but our children who haven't been raised on it or become dependent on it have no need or desire for it and would rather spend their time more wisely and constructively.

Some church programming may produce behavioral conflicts. There are many things called "Christian" which really only present ways similar to that of the world. One close home schooling friend of mine said that he was having great success with his daughter's behavior since they started home schooling. Then some friends at church persuaded them that they needed to send her to Vacation Bible School. He said that she went away well-mannered, but after two weeks, she came home a brat. Not that this is present in every church situation, but as parents we must get into the practice of evaluating such things—it will be for the good of all.

Finally, we need to consider close friends and relatives as a possible source of wrong communications. These situations are probably the most difficult in which to respond, but sometimes we are forced to set priorities with our social contacts—and such actions may at times seem unloving to others.

When parents begin to evaluate and direct the sources of communication their children are subject to, they are rightfully claiming a place of authority over their children's lives. These are two of the most important aspects to successful child rearing: 1. Discerning the content of sources of communication 2. Taking the rightful place of authority.

Proverbs 22:6 describes successful child training in this very way: "Train up a child (take the authority and responsibility) in the way he should go (direct and manage the content and sources of communication for his life): and when he is old, he will not depart from it (observe the lasting fruit of a child raised this way)."

Parental authority is becoming a lost concept today, but let's consider what God really intended and desires to see in Christian homes in this area.

2

THE PLACE OF AUTHORITY

In Scripture, we find that there are two important aspects to parental authority. Our position of authority first establishes us as an *example* to our children of God, Himself, and of proper Christian conduct and lifestyle; and, secondly, it gives us the responsibility of *instructing* our children in God's principles of life as set down in Scripture. Let me discuss these two aspects of parental authority briefly.

Parents—the Image (Example) of Christ

Much of what forms a child's perception of God will be exemplified by their parents. "Children's children are the crown of old men; and the glory of children are their fathers." Proverbs 17:6 Children tend to hold their father up as God in their little minds. This was no mistake; God intended it to be this way.

When my wife and I began to speak to our children when they were somewhere between four and seven years old about receiving Christ into their hearts, they had no reason to doubt us. There was already formed in their minds a good idea of what Christ was like as portrayed in us, their parents. We were always there...loving them...accepting them as they were...giving ourselves for them. They could trust us and believe us. It was to them as if Christ, Himself, was speaking to them.

Contrariwise, little children who have been sent away from home into the insecurity and disoriented authority structure of a school or preschool cannot comprehend what has happened in their lives. Even though parents try to reassure their children of how much fun going off to school will be, the child will reason (though it may be subconsciously) that God, represented by their parents, has pushed them away.

They feel they have fallen from the center of their parents' love and attention, and this cannot help but lessen a child's comprehension of God's deep love for them, no matter how much parents try to psyche their children up for this. This is also why they tend to show jealousy or aggression towards younger siblings that are still at home.

At this point, the child seeks desperately for someone or something to fill this authority and security void in their lives, and they usually find many sources to take this place. At a loss to see their parents as their "one" authority, they begin attaching themselves to dominant peers and many different teachers, who each have their own suggested principles of behavior and lifestyle. The child finds himself with "ten thousand instructors but not many fathers." See I Corinthians 4:15.

These children have been cheated out of having one, stable, God-ordained authority to whom they can respond. This creates a confusion in their minds which some children can adapt to more readily than others, but very few come away from this with a proper understanding of what is true God-ordained authority.

A daughter raised without having her source of authority coming mainly from her parents tends to develop an "independent spirit" and will have difficulty in adapting to the subjective role in marriage. She was not trained to see how God worked through her father for her good by being in subjection to his leadership, and now has the same problem with her husband. Her father wasn't her teacher, and, consequently, she sees little value in learning from or adapting her views and concepts of life to her husband.

The sanctifying role of her husband found in Ephesians 5:22-28 is of little value to her, for she is accustomed to having many teachers or counselors. The unity of her marriage is proportionally weak which, in turn, hinders the "grace of life" for her home. I Peter 3:7 Thus the homes of future generations are weakened.

The difficulty with sons raised under many authorities is most significantly that they may fail to see Christ as their ultimate guide and authority in life. "But I would have you know, that the head of every man is Christ." I Corinthians 11:3a They are used to having many teachers and authorities, and they can thus lose sight of their one, ultimate authority in life—God, Himself.

In such a state, they begin trying to find the most reliable or gifted teachers to follow. Many times they, unknowingly, place the authority of men or many teachers above that of God or Christ in their life. Since Christ (as represented by the father) has not been the ultimate authority in their lives, they fail to see the importance of being the ultimate authority in their own homes, and once again the home structure of future generations is weakened.

On the other hand, there are so many valuable aspects to be gained when a son is under the proper authority of both his father and mother. A son who has been taught by his mother has furthermore, through the years of his training, learned the value of the woman in a counseling position in his life. In Christian marriage, husbands are to "dwell with their wives according to knowledge" (See I Peter 3:7), to highly value and give honor to their wife's counsel on every issue of life. This is his responsibility to insure that their home is a recipient of the "grace of life."

A son who has learned to appreciate and honor his mother's counsel and has seen how God has worked through her for his good in life will readily transfer this same respect and appreciation to his future bride. Home schooling lays the foundation for successful marriage for sons and daughters.

Of course, in situations where children come from abusive, dysfunctional, or other degenerate home conditions, a child might best see Christ exemplified in a substitute authority as may be the case for orphans or other less fortunate children. But for Christian homes, the parents are to take this position, and when parents wrongfully assume someone else can just as well or better fill this position, they are creating future struggles for their child.

Parents As Teachers Of God's Word

The parental example of God's authority becomes complete when the parents take it upon themselves also to "teach" their children from God's Word. When the child sees the parents in this twofold role as "example" of God and as "teacher" of God's truth, this will have a powerful, lifelong, spiritual impact upon them.

This role of the parents (and specifically the father) as teacher of God's truth is evident throughout the Scriptures. Noah's principles of life were passed on and exemplified (taught) to his sons in the midst of a wicked generation. Abraham commanded (taught) his family after him.

God gave Moses this directive for the Children of Israel which we find recorded in Deuteronomy 6:6-7a. "And these words, which I command thee this day, shall be in thine heart: And thou shalt teach them diligently unto thy children."

And this same principle is understood for this present age being put forth in such Scriptures as Ephesians 6:4. "And, ye fathers, provoke not your children to wrath: but bring them up in the *nurture and admonition* of the Lord." Some translations render this "training and instruction of the Lord." In short, fathers (and mothers) are to be the teachers of their own children.

God has very important reasons for making "teaching fathers", for God knows, as well as anyone who has taught Biblical truth in some capacity, that generally the teacher is the one who usually learns the most. When God commanded fathers to teach their families diligently, God was wanting far more than mere intellectual assent or memory feedback of His commandments; He was expecting fathers to demonstrate and explain through everyday life situations to their children how Scripture has bearing on every aspect of life.

Fathers could demonstrate to their children throughout the day how they applied God's truth to help them in their own struggles and challenges of life, and from this, the child grasps that Scriptures are to be a light and guide for the paths of life in every area.

When Moses set down this principle in Deuteronomy 6:6-9 in which he directed fathers to diligently teach their children, God was actually setting up the father as a Bible counselor for his own home. And, of course, the wife, as the husband's "helpfit", was and is to assist and join together with her husband in this role.

Take, for example, children's literature. First of all, parents should carefully screen what their children read, even Christian literature. Once a child has read the description of something immoral, mischievous, or in some other way contrary to wholesome, Biblical conduct, this will be permanently impressed into their minds as vividly as a picture. Wise parents will guard their child's mind from certain intake.

When my wife reads with our children or when they are working a math problem or answering a history question, she encourages our children to be objective and discerning (good from evil), to look deeper into what may be subtly presented. Perhaps in a math story problem, you may read of a little girl or boy going off by themselves on their bike to buy some candy. This story may present a useful math computation, but it also presents some negatives that should be avoided such as: 1. No mention of the need to stay under parental authority and protection. 2. Presenting an independent lifestyle as normal. 3. Makes a child think that other little boys and girls are doing this without suffering evil consequences. 4. The lack of considering what is wholesome food...and there are other negatives presented in this seemingly innocent example.

The wife as a co-counselor with her husband would want to help her child evaluate and discern wherever possible from a Biblical perspective the good or the evil in what has been presented, and parents, throughout the day, should use every available opportunity to teach their children how to use wise,

Biblical discernment in every issue of life.

The instituting of various types of schools and other outside forms of instruction and adult authority directly intervenes with this principle of parental teaching. These inroads are often made gradually through philosophy and just outright deception and lies. "See to it that no one takes you captive through hollow and deceptive philosophy, which depends on human tradition and the basic principles of this world rather than on Christ." Colossians 2:8 NIV

This God-ordained position of authority granted to parents has been continually usurped and displaced by the institution. Many, many home schoolers have recognized this dilemma just as Raymond Moore has observed in one major area where this occurs—the government schools:

Remember, when you surrender your parental authority and responsibility to the state, you are still accountable for your children, but you never fully retrieve your authority. Be careful, thoughtful, and fully informed before you give away your own, lest you like others pay a price in damaged children.[3]

Almost everywhere you look today in Christianity in America, there is someone who is suppose to be better qualified to guide our families. No wonder teen-agers begin to challenge the values their father and mother try to present, for they have never been encouraged from a young age to see how God is working through their parents for their good. Until Christians begin to recognize this fundamental problem of the displaced father and mother in the child teaching and counseling process, we will see little significant improvement in the Christian home.

3

HOW PARENTS HAVE LOST THE AUTHORITY

But just how did this displacing of the God-ordained, parental authority take place, and what lies at the root of it? Does our threat come from the Communists, the Humanists, the Feminists, the Globalists...or is there something deeper behind this problem?

I assure you there is a force and a being far more subtle and powerful who has devised not only these methods but will use any means imaginable to thwart God's plan to redeem mankind and to distort and disrupt the true Biblical structure of the home. If our adversary can cause a broken marriage or lure one or more of our children from following Christ and a Biblical way of life, he has greatly hindered, if not eliminated, our testimony for Jesus Christ in the world.

Satan hates God as well as any of us who are or will be children of God. Satan would love to erase the very name of God from the face of the world, and in II Thessalonians 2:3,4 we read that Satan in the last days will attempt to do just that.

Let no man deceive you by any means: for that day shall not come, except there come a falling away first, and that man of sin (Satan) be revealed, the son of perdition; Who opposeth and exalteth himself above all that is called God, or that is worshipped; so that he as God sitteth in the temple of God, shewing himself that he is God.

From Ezekiel, we read that Satan was cast out of heaven because he wanted to be God; he wanted to have that place of authority and receive worship that only God was to receive. Satan offered Jesus all the kingdoms of the world if He would worship him...Satan wants to be worshipped. Therefore, as II Thessalonians 2:4 says, Satan will oppose anything that produces allegiance to God or anything that causes His worship. Our enemy wants to remove any reference to God or His ways from this world.

To do this, he will attack the true churches of Jesus Christ and will attempt to crumble the foundation of these churches—the strong Godly home. Satan uses philosophy to bring about these changes in society which ultimately disrupts the worship of God and erodes the unity of the home and its moral values. Public education, Humanism, and Communism really only began as philosophies that people have fallen for that bring about this end.

"Beware lest any man spoil you (lead you captive) through philosophy and vain deceit..." Colossians 2:8a It starts out as philosophy and gradually creeps into government—"Beware of the leaven of Herod..." (See Mark 8:15), and before you realize it, you have an entire nation fallen victim to this philosophy. "A little leaven (gradually) leaveneth the whole lump." Galatians 5:9 Satan also uses philosophy to disrupt true ways within the church. "Take heed, beware of the leaven of the Pharisees..."—the religious leadership. Mark 8:15

The Leaven of Herod (The Government)

Forces of evil in government have long been a problem, just as the Apostle Paul wrote in the first century A.D. "For our struggle is not against flesh and blood, but against the *rulers,* against the *authorities,* against the spiritual forces of evil in the heavenly realms." Ephesians 6:12 NIV

Satan is very cunning, and many years ago in an effort to lure children out from under parental guidance, training, and authority, he observed a way that this could be done. If he could somehow convince parents through philosophy and vain deceit that they are going to do an inferior job at training their children—academically and spiritually—then parents will voluntarily give up this God-given role. With the resulting loss and belittling of the teaching father and mother and with the lack of loyalty and respect that the children will begin to have, it will be only a matter of time before the family structure begins to deteriorate. Ultimately Biblical values then become unimportant to society, God's ways and standards are lost sight of, and instead of people now worshipping and serving God, they will readily accept a substitute to worship and serve.

Satan usually moves in gradually to do this, making his efforts appear as good works. The first public (government) schools were started in Boston where they really were not even needed. Over 90% of school age children were being schooled in some way voluntarily already, many of them at home. But in an effort to compel the very small percentage who were not attending some form of schooling to do so, they gradually enacted laws which forced everyone to attend for fear that the few who were not would soon become our cities' criminals.

The forefathers of these same men in New England also had enacted laws to force everyone to attend church, thinking this would somehow make everybody a Christian! The following is an excerpt from the Connecticut Blue Laws of 1650.

It is ordered and decreed by this court and authority thereof, that wheresoever the ministry of the Word is established, according to the order of the gospel, throughout this jurisdiction, every person shall duly resort and attend thereunto respectively upon the Lord's Day...after due means of conviction used, he shall forfeit for his absence, from every such public meeting, 5 shillings.[4]

We are sadly aware today that similarly compulsory education laws in America certainly do not guarantee that everyone is free from crime, successful, reasonably educated, or even literate! But Satan recognized that, by barrages of philosophy presented through his puppets over many years of time, people would gradually fall for this idea. Marxism is certainly an obvious example of this.

Because of false philosophy, there are very few today in America who would begin to challenge the value of compulsory education; and there are also few Christians who have ever recognized how Satan has used compulsory education to snatch our children away from us in the years when they are the most vulnerable.

In fact, it was so-called "Christians" who actually came up with this "good work" in the first place. Once people become convinced that certain practices are the so-called "right" thing to do in society, it is rather easy to get someone to activate laws requiring everyone's submission to these ways.

There are also many unwritten laws that we voluntarily submit to and obey unknowingly. If everyone we are associated with is following certain, unwritten policies for their lives, one suddenly becomes a lawbreaker or rebel if he chooses not to follow such practices.

For example, when I began to talk to some of my close, Christian friends about home schooling in the mid-70's, I suddenly found myself being looked upon as a heretic, or at least my Biblical reasoning for doing so was in error. After all, not one of our leaders in our Christian circles was considering such an idea; however, I was familiar with the children of many of these leaders and recognized the struggles their parents were facing with them. Even after several years, many of these same people recognized the success we were having with home schooling our children—yet they were still unwilling to contribute this to our determination to bring our children up in unconventional ways. It's time we begin to realize that there may not be safety in numbers.

Moses, when attempting to lead the Children of Israel out of Egypt so that they could worship and serve God in the way that God desired, was confronted with this proposition from Pharaoh:

So Moses and Aaron were brought back to Pharaoh. "All right, go and serve Jehovah your God!" he said. "But just who is it you want to go?" "We will go with our sons and

daughters, flocks and herds," Moses replied. *"We will take everything with us; for we must all join in the holy pilgrimage." "In the name of God I will not let you take your little ones!" Pharaoh retorted. "I can see your plot! Never! You that are men, go and serve Jehovah, for that is what you asked for."*
Exodus 10:8-10 The Living Bible

Moses found himself here in a situation where he was forced to wrestle against spiritual wickedness in places of authority when trying to reason with Pharaoh (the government). Satan is wise and has the ability to see beyond the present generation into the future. He is not so concerned if we adults find satisfaction in our religious life as long as he knows he has our children away from our effective influence for God, and in an environment where he can erode away their faith and moral values.

This is why many of the leaders in the home schooling movement have recognized that their ultimate goal in home education is to "...raise up the foundations of many Godly generations."[5]

Pharaoh was not willing to allow this process of preparing future Godly generations to take place in his day. The government has likewise attempted to prevent this in America today.

The early common schools were the original public schools started in New England, but prior to the American Revolution, many towns had no common schools at all.

Home education was a major form, if not the predominant form, of education in Colonial America and in the early years after the adoption of the Constitution.[6]

In fact the U.S. Constitution does not even mention education, and the reason is rather obvious—our founding fathers recognized that parents were in the best place to determine the content and extent of their child's education, not the government. This was their parental right and responsibility. However, Satan recognized the potential the locally supported, common schools had in his being able to creep in and gradually take control of the children, and he used a small minority of individuals who had drifted from true, Biblical Christianity as instruments in bringing about this scheme. (See *N.E.A.-Trojan Horse in American Education* by Samuel L. Blumenfeld, Chapter 1-"How We Got Public Education.")

We must not forget how much our adversary hated the religious fervor and devotion to Jesus Christ so many early Americans had. Benjamin Franklin, in his autobiography, described the religious climate in Philadelphia in the early 1740's this way: "It seemed as if all the world were growing religious, so that one could not walk through the town in an evening without hearing psalms sung in different families of every street."

Notice that the families were worshipping and praising God as a unit; unfortunately, this was gradually to be changed. The government's heart, with whom we now must wrestle to reclaim the rearing of our children, has once again been hardened just as it was in the days of Moses.

> *Then Pharaoh summoned Moses and said, "Go worship the Lord. Even your women and children may go with you..." "But the Lord hardened Pharaoh's heart, and he was not willing to let them go."*
>
> Exodus 10:24 & 27

My wife had her Degree in Education with distinction from a leading university in our state and had taught in the public schools, being highly recommended. I thought it would be a rather simple thing for us to gain permission for her to teach our son at home. After all, there wasn't a school district around that wouldn't have hired her to teach 30 or 40 youngsters. Why should they object to her teaching just one at home? This was in the mid-1970's. (My wife points out that you didn't then nor do you now need a teacher's degree to home school. Some of the most advanced home schooled children we know have been taught by parents who are high school educated.)

I called the school official in that state (we have since moved) and related to him our intentions, but he said that if we insisted on home schooling, they would soon have us in court. We quickly realized that we were going to have to wrestle with evil that had somehow crept into the government. I thought this type of family intervention was only happening at that time in Soviet Russia and not in America!

We see basically two Biblical choices when faced with these situations of confrontation with evil in government. The first is to resist and appeal their demands. Sometimes evil in government has happened because Satan has crept in and presented a practice which is not truly God-ordained—like in Haman's wicked plot to destroy the Jews in Esther's day. Esther's appeal and stand against the scheme averted the outcome of the plot.

But there are other times when evil in government is simply to be avoided by some means. For example, God certainly could have struck down Herod so that Joseph wouldn't have needed to take the child Jesus and his mother and flee into Egypt, but He didn't. Instead, they just moved away, and this eventually resulted in them moving to Nazareth, so that Jesus could be called a Nazarene in fulfillment of Scripture. Jesus also chose not to minister in certain cities which had rejected him. Sometimes govermental situations that have become evil make a Biblical lifestyle impossible to follow—at least for a time.

These are times of prayer, but we must believe that if the government remains unyielding to our requests upon prayer and a time of waiting, that certainly God has a better plan for us. We forsook all to home school and moved to a more favorable state. This move was one of special blessing for our marriage and family unity, and for our faith and spiritual life as well. This ended up being a wonderful life changing choice for us.

The Leaven of Pharisees (Religious Leadership)

The Pharisees were the dominant, ruling, religious leaders in Christ's day. Jesus told the common people to "hear them but don't be like them." For the most part, Scripture reading was only available at the local synogogues—this is why they were to "hear them." But the synogogues were under the Pharisees' control, and the Pharisees were not good examples to follow. Jesus warned his disciples to be wary of the leaven of these predominant religious leaders.

The word leaven in the Bible is used to describe evil, corruption, or deterioration of righteous principles. A little leaven gradually leavens the whole lump. This is why Christians are encouraged to abhor that which is evil and to abstain from all appearance of evil—because a little evil will, in time, spread throughout the group, and then this evil, which was once obvious, becomes commonplace and acceptable. Now that the group has become desensitized to this evil, the adversary can introduce something a little more evil and so on until the group is no longer distinctively more righteous than the world around them.

Jesus' teachings and the soon to follow New Testament Scriptures took a large part of the spiritual teaching away from the religious leaders and put the truth back into the hands of the common people. Paul taught that those who were to be leaders in the early church were first to be able to "rule their own houses well" and be "apt" to teach. See I Timothy 3:1-7.

They were to be able to skillfully apply Scripture to those everyday life issues at home with their family, and this, in turn, would prepare them to be able to take "care of the church" or teach larger numbers. Most of the problems encountered in managing a church body are very similar to those found in managing one's own home. Christianity grew rapidly under this plan, and the foundations of future Godly generations were established.

Gradually, with the influx of Roman Catholicism, Satan through religious leadership once again was wresting the instruction of the family from the hands of the fathers and putting it into the hands of a more "enlightened" few. This diabolical plan has lasted for many years and was responsible for bringing about the "Dark Ages."

But with the advent of the Protestant Reformation beginning in the mid-fourteenth to fifteenth centuries by men like Wycliffe and Huss, Calvin, Zwingli, and Luther, the Bible was translated and encouraged to be read and applied by the common people.

Fathers once again became the spiritual leaders—not the Priests or the Pope. Christianity began to flourish, and on into the seventeenth and eighteenth centuries, the revival fires were burning brightly in Europe and the New World.

But the one who deceives the nations will not give up his thrusts until God does away with him. So we can be sure that he will constantly be devising means whereby he may disrupt or discount the need for the teaching home.

There is an endless availability of Bible teaching in America today, accessible at local churches two or three times a week, as well as through seminars, radio teaching, books, tapes, Bible studies, and on and on; yet, for some strange reason, most fathers feel incompetent to teach their own families. Could it be that our adversary would cunningly use this assortment of knowledge to make fathers feel it is unneedful to teach basic Bible truth at home? Subtle philosophy can so easily convince us fathers (and also our wives and children) that there is a better teacher who is more professional, better educated, or more gifted to instruct our families.

Intellectual, Biblical, head knowledge has become a substitute for the wise application of Scripture to challenges in our daily walk—which God has ordained fathers to teach their children. Many fathers today are beginning to retake their position as spiritual leader and guide to their homes. God has not only ordained them to do so, but he has and will equip them for the task.

Subtle Philosophy

Our adversary will make every attempt to compel Christian parents to place their children in group-oriented schooling or social situations. He knows children will begin to compromise—if not morally, they will certainly fail to perceive how peer pressure has altered their lifestyle. Gregg Harris points out how subtly this progressive, peer influence and worldly drift can so easily infect our children.

The child tends to hold to the norms and values of his peer group, over and above those of the parental team. When faced with a conflict between the standards of his parents and those of his peers at school, the child seeks ways to meet the group's demands without provoking discipline from his parents....His tastes in dress, hair, music, food, toys, and vocabulary fall into line with his group's standards. Less noticeable are changes in the child's attitude toward family standards in faith and morality.

Once the child's tastes are being heavily affected by his group, the child tends to become a victim of more deep-seated, social contagion. Various behaviors and vocabulary are freely passed around the group. Leaders in the peer group, often the most rebellious to begin with, start testing their powers over each member by asking outlandish things of them. The choice is always the same: conform or be rejected.[7]

A recent pole by a leading Christian magazine has indicated that among Christian families in America, eight out of ten of their children are forsaking the faith and being lost to worldliness. Sadly the ones we usually hear praised and exemplified in our churches are those one or two out of ten who do follow the faith. Christian parents would recognize more readily how ineffective the conventional public and church schooled child rearing methods are if they were more honest and open about the vast number of failures.

Before Christian parents will yield up their children, they must be convinced that this is the right thing to do. This is where philosophy comes in, and this is why the Apostle Paul admonishes us to beware of the philosophy and deceptions behind issues of life. "Beware lest any man spoil you (lead you or your children captive) through philosophy and vain deceit, after the tradition of men, after the rudiments of the world, and not after Christ." Col. 2:8

The children of Israel were first philosophized into thinking they needed a king before they asked for one. "Now make us a king to judge us like all the other nations." I Samuel 8:5b

They observed the way the rest of the world had a king to fight their battles and run their countries, and they falsely concluded that this was best for them. They were philosophized into following the "rudiments", the basic ways, of the world voluntarily.

God, through the prophet, Samuel, tried to point out the fallacies in their reasoning and showed them what would be the consequences of their wishes.

And he said, This will be the manner of the king that shall reign over you: He will take your sons, and appoint them for himself...and he will take your daughters (and so on)...And ye shall cry out in that day because of your king which ye shall have chosen you; and the Lord will not hear you in that day. Nevertheless the people refused to obey the voice of Samuel; and they said, Nay; but we will have a king over us.
I Samuel 8:11,13,18 & 19

In God's sight, what they wanted to do was wrong, but because it was socially acceptable and everyone else in the world was doing it, they went ahead. Now God used it eventually for the good, but remember it was not the best way from the beginning.

The sad reality is that not only the government but also many well-meaning, yet misinformed Christians will attempt to convince you that you shouldn't take your God-given place of authority and leadership over your children. They have been philosophized into thinking that your authority should be given to the government, the church, or others; and many will not want you to home school because your example will become convicting to them.

4

TAKING THE AUTHORITY

Recently we invited a young couple who was interested in home schooling over for dinner. We knew the father was ready to start home schooling at once, but the wife was having reservations. We thought perhaps his wife was feeling incompetent because she was high school educated and had no teaching experience, and my wife wanted to lay to rest any fears the woman might have had. My wife described to the mother the many available materials and curricula, trying to reassure her that she was more than adequately qualified.

After conversation at length, the wife smiled and whispered, "Oh, I know I can do it, but just don't tell anybody." My wife could sense that the real problem wasn't the mother feeling capable to teach her children—but more the problem of being able to control them and a willingness to make the necessary changes in her lifestyle to take the authority over her children.

Actually, both of these concerns are unfounded. Many children seem like they will be uncontrollable at home because they have spent the better part of each day away from home in an environment where they are more or less uncontrolled; this usually isn't the case in home schooling once things begin to get organized and supervised properly. Most home schooling mothers also soon find the home-oriented lifestyle to be more accommodating than before to the Lord's work once priorities are rearranged.

Much of the negative behavior children display at home is picked up at school and reinforced there on a daily basis. When this negative chain of exposure is broken, a large part of misbehavior will begin to subside in a relatively short period of time. Soon your child will begin to act differently just by being at home—provided that you minimize their exposure to improper conduct which may be found in other sources like playmates, church situations, friends, relatives, TV, videos, books, etc.

Turning the Hearts of the Fathers

Many potential home schooling mothers also react at the thought of the additional burden this will add to an already busy life. Home schooling and child training are very much men's work, too. The father, above all, should take the lead and authority in this work.

One of the signs of the imminent return of Christ in the last days is this increasing burden in the hearts of the fathers to be turned to their own children.

> *Behold, I will send you Elijah the prophet before the coming of the great and dreadful day of the Lord: And he shall turn the heart of the fathers to the children, and the heart of the children to their fathers, lest I come and smite the earth with a curse. Malachi 4:5,6*

It is best for husbands and wives to be involved in this work together as "heirs together" as much as possible in order to see God's blessing upon this ministry. Husbands may need to alter involvements and careers to find the time to give themselves properly for this work. It has only been in recent years historically that most fathers have been involved in employment away from home.

I pulled out of a big business opportunity I had when my children were young and started a very small and meager business at home where I could be more available and more directly involved with our children's training. I admit, it was difficult financially for years, though we always had enough; but eventually God prospered my small home occupation and has given me the opportunity to apprentice my own children in this work. I can only say this...God will surely bless a father who is willing to give himself first for the needs of his wife and children.

It is valuable for the father to take the oversight and discernment in every issue in the home, not only with school curricula and child training principles, but with many of those everyday encounters in life. Daily communication between the husband and wife is perhaps the most important key to this. My wife and I have a communication time at breakfast together before the day begins and again in the evening where we discuss particular needs, burdens, behavior situations with the children, involvements, and activities—trying to discern the will of the Lord together.

Many times wives can find their lives becoming excessively burdened and may have difficulty knowing why. Sometimes just a little too much extra activity in life can make everything seem very heavy or confusing. Wives will be surprised at the comfort and guidance they will receive as God works through their husband in helping them discern together the needs for her life and the home. A husband's heart cannot be termed "turned" to his children unless it is first "turned" to his wife and her needs.

The same is true for the husband's life. Wives can sometimes detect situations that are making his life stressful or overly involved, and wives can also sense when the children need some special time with their father. Remember, our first real ministry for Christ is found in our own homes. Our dedication and commitment to this work will have much to say regarding our future service for Christ.

Be creative in finding these husband and wife communication times together. We know of one home schooling couple who have part of their communication time in taking an evening walk together up and down their driveway within calling distance of the children. "Mother's Night Out" is a part of our home life, but instead of mom going out by herself, my wife and I enjoy this time together. The world makes mothers think they need a break from their children, and there is some validity to this; but it should be done in proper and Godly ways. Rather than driving somewhere by herself, my wife prefers that we go together and either have dinner or do some shopping for family needs. We have also used these special times together as an opportunity to minister to the spiritual needs of others or to go witnessing together.

Taking The Authority Brings Respect

I have heard mothers argue, "I don't think I can gain the respect my children give to their teachers at school." Do you know why teachers manage to have to some extent this control and respect? It is simply because they *take* the position of authority over the children. They have respect because they expect respect, and if you as a parent assume this same role and attitude of authority over your child at home, *you will* experience having the same respect. Just take the authority, and you have taken a giant step towards gaining control.

Take the lead and say, "This is what we are going to do today." You have the God-given right as well as the responsibility to set the standards and direct the actions of your child. Once you decide you are going to be the leader and authority, your children will begin to fall in line under this authority. Now, of course, you will face rebellion against this authority from time to time, but I deal with this subject in more detail later.

In addition to expecting respect, a school teacher in a classroom situation also daily regulates the child's time, giving them something to do. This is important especially for younger children somewhere before the age of 12; they are incapable of planning their own day, and someone needs to help them do this. When your child sees you *taking the authority over them* and also *helping them organize their day and directing their activities,* they sense that someone really cares for them. This is why children often have a fondness for a teacher at school—

this teacher has met two of their most basic needs.

But when parents forfeit the educating (and training) of their children, they have given up one of the most fulfilling and useful ways there is in building family love and unity and true Godly character. Home school gives you and your child something very useful and purposeful to do together which will help them develop this same respect and fondness for you the parent. When this responsibility is given over to someone else, there is literally very little else you can do with or for your child. It's like having someone else feed your child three meals a day... and then expecting your child to enjoy or desire the meal you have prepared for them—someone else has already met their basic needs.

So often as parents we really have no daily plans for our child except play, or trying to figure out various forms of entertainment, and children tend to get tired of that. They like and need to have some useful things to do too. One of the virtues of the New Testament mother is that she is to "guide the household." I Timothy 5:14 This is why so many women aspire to be school teachers, for they have this inner desire to guide something and to teach. God has given mothers this ability to be used first in their own homes. Don't let the world distract you with its substitutes from this fullfilling first work for Christ.

Make plans for your child's day with righteousness in mind and select your curriculum based on the Godliness of its content. (You may need to mix portions from different suppliers). Steer your child away from TV and other sources of uncreative entertainment, and rather guide and encourage them to use their free time more productively in activities like practicing music, hobbies and crafts that develop manual and artistic skills, and homemaking skills, etc. Young boys profit from toys and projects that encourage and enhance mechanical knowledge. Parents need to be creative together in suggesting the kinds of activities that would be best for their children. Little work assignments not only build a servant's spirit in your child but will instill in them the value of using time wisely.

Social Dependency and Taking the Authority with Respect to Playmates

If you are beginning to feel uncomfortable with the influence some other children may be having on yours, then politely withdraw your child. We have moved out of neighborhoods and avoided certain social situations in order to keep our children from constant exposure to negative examples.

It is the world that has led us to believe that children have to have other children their own age to play with if they are going to enjoy themselves. This idea has come out of the age-segregated, classroom lifestyle of most institutionally raised children. For our own family, we have always encouraged our children to play together with brothers and sisters. We have never feared the outcome of this because they each know the rules and attitudes that we allow and accept, and we further feel it has been valuable for our children to be held accountable for their behavior by each other. If encouraged in this way by you, the parents, your children will feel very fulfilled with the companionship of a brother or sister in a relatively short period of time. Here, again, it's the world that has taught that this isn't possible.

I remember my wife and I remarking to each other of how much fun our then nineteen and twelve-year-old sons were having working together on some pieces of furniture they were building. It has given me great joy several times walking back to our small barn and hearing my eleven and fourteen-year-old daughters and thirteen-year-old son talking joyfully while cooperatively straightening up the barn together and taking care of the animals.

Our children also look forward to a family play night usually at least once a week. There has been many a Friday night around our house when a vigorous game of "Capture the Flag," ice skating on the pond, or a horse-drawn wagon or sleigh ride has been followed by an adventure-virtue story told in the family room. Storytelling can convey many wholesome principles while being sure the content doesn't present something objectionable that you wish your children hadn't heard or seen. Psalm 90 talks about a tale that is told. It doesn't take a lot of ability for father to tell a simple virtue story.

One word of caution about siblings playing together. It is much easier to be disobedient when you have a companion who supports or, at least, doesn't challenge your disobedience. In the past when we have seen one of our children supporting wrong behavior or attitudes in another, we knew it was time for them to be separated and to find something to do on their own for a while. Some children, like adults, seem to be more dependent on others to enjoy themselves, but sometimes children just need encouragement in being able to learn to play or work creatively alone. "Study to be quiet, and to do your own business, and to work with your own hands, as we commanded you." I Thes. 4:11

We feel that the best friendship associations are found through social involvements with other families rather than encouraging our children to be involved individually with others or in activities which would tend to separate family unity.

I don't believe it's wise to let children go off and play in the neighborhood. We moved out of the neighborhood into the country because our children were continually being vexed and tempted by the mischief other children in our neighborhood were presenting to them. If your children are not troubled with such associations, then you can be sure they are learning to compromise with or conform to the ways of the world to some degree. "And be not conformed to this world: but be ye transformed..." Romans 12:2a

Someone might say, "It's easy for your children to enjoy playing together because you have five, but we only have one." I think an only child, or say two children, are just as privileged because, believe it or not, most children wish their mother or father was their closest companion. There is great comfort in this relationship once children (and parents) learn proper ways. A lot of children just give up hope in having this close relationship with parents because parents are too preoccupied with something else or others.

Give It Some Time

Some parents start home schooling and home training their children only to give up after the first year. Remember when you had your first child? That first year there were so many times you didn't know what to expect, or what was normal, or whether things would some day get easier, and you didn't need to have a degree in child bearing or previous experience to do all right. But you made it through; and by the time your second child came along, it was much easier. You knew more of what to expect. It is a lot like this your first year of home schooling. But by the second year, you've gained a lot of experience, and by the third year, you probably could write a book about it.

Richard Fugate, author of *What the Bible Says About...Child Training*, shares this about parental authority:

As a human authority, you will make many mistakes even if you desire to be right and just. These mistakes can be from ignorance of what or how to deal with children, or they can be a result of sin. An authority does not have to be perfect in his rulership. Obedience and respect for the power of rulership is often learned from what appears to be unfair or incompetent leadership. Parents, you are the authority—right or wrong! Do not allow the fact that you are human and subject to error hinder you from meeting your responsibilities. God knew you were imperfect when He gave you a child. The recognition of this fact should make you dependent on Him, not cause you to avoid the responsibility.[8]

Begin to Expect Obedience

As you assume your role of authority, try to get into the habit of expecting your child to do as you ask instead of having their option to do as you ask. When you give a child their option, they can choose not to be under your direction. Later on, once you have securely gained your position of authority and the child begins to respect that position, the rules can be loosened up a little, and the child can be given more of a choice.

Also bear in mind that most group-schooled children are not really taught to respect authority; rather they learn how to get around authority because their primary response is towards their peers. So if your child spends much time with wrong examples in this area of authority, they may very well begin to learn how to "look" like they respect your leadership but do not in their heart. Once we decide to take the rightful and God-ordained position of authority over our children, we must begin to evaluate all the sources of "evil communications" (I Cor. 15:33) by which the child is influenced.

It is one thing to assume our rightful place of authority and leadership over our children, but it's another to bring them under control and mold them into respectful, obedient children who are in "subjection with all gravity." I Timothy 3:4

Half the battle is just bringing them home and taking the authority—the other half is shaping their behavior so that it becomes a delight to spend each day with your children. "The father of the righteous shall greatly rejoice: and he that begetteth a wise child shall have joy of him." Prov. 23:24 In the following chapters, let's see how the parents can begin this process of shaping their child's behavior.

5

GAINING CONTROL THROUGH ONE REQUIREMENT

God knew that child training wouldn't be easy, and so He has given parents one central principle which, if wisely and diligently applied and followed, would enable them to see success. This principle was first set down in the Ten Commandments, and its application is expanded in Col. 3:20- "Children, obey your parents in *all* things: for this is well pleasing unto the Lord." Similarly we read in Eph. 6:1,2 and 3- "Children, obey your parents in the Lord: for this is right. Honour thy father and mother which is the first commandment with promise."

The promise in verse 3 which is taken from the Ten Commandments is this: "That it may be well with thee, and thou mayest live long on the earth." In short, this principle of child training is simply requiring your child to obey you in all things with an honoring attitude so that life will go well for your child.

Parents: God's Representatives

These Scriptures were first of all and above all written for parents; it was the parents' duty to see that their children followed this commandment. God has required that children obey their parents, and when we require our children to do so, we are acting in God's behalf. We have His authority.

Most parents want the best for their children. They want life, in general, to "go well" for their child, and, of course, they would like to see their child live a "long" blessed life. This promise in Eph. 6:1-3 expressly offers this to the child who has been trained by his parents to have an honoring attitude towards mother and father, and this honoring attitude is particularly evidenced by his obedience to his parents during those younger years.

God did not want to encumber or confuse parents by giving them numerous regulations regarding child training, so He put forth this one, all encompassing principle of children obeying their parents in all things to simplify our goal.

The Subject of the Will of a Child

A child cannot be termed as obedient to his parents with an honoring attitude unless his will is subject to theirs. Therefore, as we begin to talk about children obeying their parents in all things so that it will go well for them, we are at the same time talking about the child having a subjective will. "If ye be willing and obedient, ye shall eat the good of the land." Isaiah 1:19 The will and obedience go hand-in-hand.

All children are willfull to some extent because all parents are willful to some extent; it is an inherent part of human nature. Jesus is the only Man who could fully say, "My meat is to do the will of Him that sent me..." John 4:34 and, "Nevertheless, not my will but thine be done." Luke 22:42b He had a perfectly subjective will to His heavenly Father as well as to His earthly parents.

As Christian adults and parents, our goal is to learn to subject our wills to the will of God, our proper authority; and we, in turn, can give our child a head start in this process by teaching them to willingly obey their parents in all things.

On the other hand, if we take lightly this task of teaching our children to obey us as their authority, we are subconsciously instilling in them the concept that God's will can be lightly esteemed. Eli took lightly his responsibility in making his sons obey him when they were younger; consequently, upon reaching manhood when they were too old to be restrained, they assumed that God had this same attitude towards them which they had seen exemplified to them when being raised by their father. "...His sons made themselves vile, and he restrained them not." I Samuel 3:13b

Eli did try rebuking his sons when they were older, but their willful, self-gratifying lifestyle had already been thoroughly set in them.

> *Nay, my sons: for it is no good report that I hear; ye make the Lord's people to transgress. If one man sin against another, the judge shall judge him: but if a man sin against the Lord, who shall entreat for him? Not withstanding, they hearkened not unto the voice of their father, because the Lord would slay them."* I Samuel 2:24, 25

It is very important as parents to begin training our children to obey us as early as possible in their lives, for it is much easier to nip behavioral conflicts in the bud before they are in full bloom. It makes life much more bearable for all.

Even an infant can be seen to exert their will above your will when they display such things as kicking, defiance, anger, or stubbornness when you go to do something like change a diaper or make them sit still on your lap. These may be some forms of their first attempts to challenge you and see if you are going to make them obey you "in all things." Get into the habit of discerning when your child is trying to set their will above yours. This is your way of measuring the extent of their obedience to you.

For example, take an infant who is just learning to walk or perhaps is still crawling. While being held, he or she attempts to wriggle or squirm free to get down. Don't allow them to get their way, but insist that your will be done. Hold them firmly and calmly tell them no. As the child persists in getting their way, remain determined to win the conflict of wills and don't yield. After a few attempts at this, your child will discover the futility of his efforts and will gradually dismiss this behavior.

A word of caution about "evil communications" corrupting

good manners may be needed. If you as a parent are continuously delegating the care of your child to those like grandparents, friends, older siblings, nursery attendants, etc., who may yield to your child's desire to squirm free and get down, then you are teaching your child a double standard. You are saying to your child, "There are times when you must be obedient, and there are times for willfulness."

This doesn't end with infancy, for as this child becomes older, he learns to put on the right show at the right times. Then, when a teen-ager, this same child may make the mistake of running with his own will and seeking companionship with those who support his views. However, if, from an early age, we insist and demonstrate the value of our child submitting to the will of their proper authorities, they will be prone to submit to the Lord's authority and His righteousness for their lives when older.

Delighting To Do God's Will

"I delight to do thy will, O my God..."
Psalm 40:8—written by David.

David was a man after God's own heart, and this was primarily so because he desired to do all of God's will. Unlike his predecessor, King Saul, David was obedient to the will and authority of God. This principle of learning to delight in doing God's will is actually what parents are instilling in their children when they begin requiring their children at a young age to have parental permission and approval before doing things.

When you require your child to sit still on your lap until *you* decide it's time for them to get down, you are beginning to teach this concept. When you require your toddler to hold your hand when walking down the sidewalk or when out in public places, you are continuing to teach this truth. When they learn to obey simple commands like "No touch," they are in the early stages of this training. When you require your child to stay with you instead of wandering off at will into another room, you are preventing not only willfulness but also an independent nature and spirit from developing in the child.

Encouraging your child to play quietly, not to be boisterous or too talkative, and learning that there are times to be quiet and not to ask questions, etc., help them learn this subjective role and also lay the preliminaries for controlling their whole bodies with its fleshly demands. See James 3:2.

However, we cannot expect too much in this way from young children. We didn't send our children off to a nursery, but neither did we expect them to sit through a two or three hour church service. We did train our children to sit quietly for periods of time; and even as toddlers, they would sit through a service if we wanted them to. Some parents falsely justify that they can require their young children to sit through lengthy meetings if they allow them to "let off steam" in between or afterwards; rather, it is better for the parents to gauge their involvements according to what their children's ages and training can accommodate.

We have found that it is better not to let one extreme justify another. This may seem trivial, but this teaching lies at the center of self-control. When a child is taught that they should sit quietly for two or three hours and can then run wild afterwards, they are being conditioned to have behavioral "swings." This then affects other areas of their life. After they have been trained to think, "I will behave myself while Mom and Dad are around, but in a little while I can run wild with my playmates," they can begin to reason, "I will eat a light lunch so I can indulge myself at dinner," or "I will restrain myself with my spending for a while so that I can splurge later." Try to encourage more of an even keel in your child's behavior, attitudes, and habits.

The Terrible Two's Myth

Contrary to what many are led to believe, your toddler does not have to pass through a particularly difficult stage of child training around the age of two, three, or four. This is merely the age when a child's little mind has developed sufficiently to enable them to more effectively set their will at odds with their parents' will. They are becoming more aware of things going on around them. Hopefully, by this age, the parents have, to some extent, trained this child's will to respond to their commands. Of course, if the parent has neglected to consistently set their will over their child's will up to this point, the "terrible twos" are going to seem terrible, indeed.

Around this age from two to four, the parents will have frequent opportunities to see that their child's will is subject to theirs in everything. This requires constant supervision and diligence at this age level, and makes the years following this period much more enjoyable; but neglect will make the years following difficult if not unbearable.

Older siblings who display subjective, obedient wills towards their parents can build their own discernment in this area of the will by parents allowing the younger brothers and sisters to be held accountable to their older brothers and sisters. There is an "old wive's tale" going around that older children that report to the parents on the behavior and attitude of younger siblings are somehow in violation of Scripture and are "tattlers." This isn't true.

Of course, parents will need to discern in given situations the circumstances involved, but parents usually know when an older brother or sister is being responsible and only reporting for the good of their younger sibling. This is very much a concept for the church. The younger are to submit to the elder and are to be subject (accountable) one to another. See I Peter 5:5.

Respect for older brothers and sisters as well as respect sisters have towards brothers and vice versa are important building blocks for Godly living. Some young children think that they can be respectful and obedient to their parents and at the same time be disrespectful to brothers and sisters. However, in truth, the younger child is not genuinely developing respect from their heart; they are only performing what has to be done to make a "show" of respect to their parents while being allowed to have an unloving and disrespectful attitude towards others.

If you are going to delegate the supervision of your toddler or youngster to an older brother or sister, it will be necessary for the parent to stand behind this older sibling and minister the necessary punishment accordingly. Older brothers and sisters can be very helpful in correcting improper attitudes in younger children.

Judgment with Love

It is interesting to note that just as God gave children one command in the New Testament Age of obeying their parents in all things, He also gave Adam and Eve one commandment to not eat of the tree of the knowledge of good and evil in the Garden. When they did eat of this forbidden tree, God did two things. First, He demonstrated His displeasure with their actions by the subsequent curse, but at the same time He offered love and provision for their now sinful nature. He demonstrated judgment for their actions coupled with love and forgiveness.

A young child should be handled in a similar way by their parents. A child who displays stubbornness, willfulness, or defiance (perhaps squirming to get down, etc.) should be held firmly while the parent indicates their displeasure with their child's *actions* by firmly saying, "No! No! Mother (or Father) says No! No!" Continue this until the child yields up their will to yours. Then verbalize your pleasure with their new, yielded attitude. Take them into your arms and demonstrate your love and forgiveness to them. Judgment with love and forgiveness must go together.

It is important to not have a rejecting spirit towards a child for negative behavior (putting them in their room alone is a mild form of rejection). By rejecting a child for their misbehavior, we are causing them to reason that God rejects us for sinful behavior. God *is* displeased with our sins, but once we have repented (yielded our will to Him), He freely offers us His love and forgiveness. He doesn't reject us.

Psalms 66:18 says that God does not hear the prayers of sinners; God does reject us as sinners until we repent. Children isolated as punishment (sent to their room, etc.) can be warmly welcomed back when they repent. They should be informed, however, that the temporary rejection was a result of their misbehavior only and that we still very much love them. This form of punishment does have certain limitations as to its effectiveness with some children and can often inadvertently become an easy way out of taking the sometimes necessary effort to spank or correct the child.

Rejection can be very devastating to a child and to adults, alike. This is why peer pressure has such an influence on children, because they disdain the rejection of the group. Being "put out of the synagogue" (social rejection) was something that was very disgraceful to any adult Jew in Christ's day, and social ostracism is a powerful tool in causing individuals to conform to the practices of the group.

Regularly putting a child into the insecurity of a noisy nursery or when older on a school bus can be equated in their little minds to some extent with rejection, no matter how much we try to convince them otherwise. These can be discouraging times for a child, because they often subconsciously reason that the one who loves me the most and the one I love the most and feel the most secure with is sending me away for some reason.

Begin today expecting your child to obey you in "all things" in everything you request of them. If you ask your child to do something and they don't respond in obedience, or if they have neglected to do something that is expected of them, then inform them of the importance God places on their obedience to you the parents—"that it may be well with them" in life, etc.

Point out the Biblical importance behind your request, and encourage them to obey God's words, which are your requests also. This will begin to train a child at a young age of the value in having a Scriptural basis for their actions in life.

Now, of course, there are going to be times when they refuse to obey your request, and there will often be times when it will be necessary to take stronger measures to see that they comply, but I will have more to say about these measures in subsequent chapters.

6

UNDERSTANDING WILLFULNESS

Every child is willful to some degree, and some can be very strong willed; but it is also rare that the first-born is overly willful. Usually the first-born is more compliant in nature, although they are still willful somewhat. God is very gracious and understanding in making it this way, and He knows that inexperienced parents need practice in dealing with the will (obedience) of their children. God thus gives parents in their first-born an opportunity to learn how to deal with a child's will before perhaps a more difficult child may come along.

An excessively angry child (one who may display temper tantrums) is a child who has not had his or her will restrained when younger. A child who has temper tantrums is simply a child who has (when a little older) been restrained or restricted from getting what they were use to getting. Their anger has become an effective tool for this child to manipulate their own way or will in things.

But if parents start out early not giving their child his or her every wish and demand, they can train their child not to expect things to always go the way the child wants. A child's wishes can grow into demands rather quickly if we're not careful.

Meeting Needs

We can, however, be unknowingly training our child to be

willful or demanding because we have not met their basic needs. A dirty diaper can be unpleasant to an infant; it may develop into a rash if it isn't attended to promptly, and a rash can make an infant even more demanding (wanting our comfort).

It is also impossible to tell a hungry infant they are on a three or four hour feeding schedule. To them they have a need which demands our attention. Frequent small feedings are the rule in some cultures (you may want to check with your physician); however, we have found that gentle cradling of the infant in our arms often satisfies this need.

Insecurity in infants manifested by such problems as crying out or screaming in the night and excessive fear in being left alone during the day (or night) can be caused by several factors. In general, a peaceful night can be expected to follow a peaceful day. Confusion caused by having radios, television, children's videos, disorderly siblings or playmates, a mother's inattentiveness during the day, nurseries, daycare, and babysitters can all contribute to this problem. Attention to these areas along with the idea of keeping the cradle or crib in Dad and Mom's bedroom until baby feels secure in being alone is a good idea.

If basic needs like these aren't attended to, then we inadvertently can be training our child to be demanding and to use many means to promote the parental response.

Discernment in the Area of Food Preferences

As the infant progresses from milk to soft foods, new training in this area of the will begins, and a baby may differentiate between foods liked or disliked. We tried to make it a point for our children to eat what Father and Mother wished, even if peas didn't taste as good as plums. This can be a little challenging as you may know, but the point is that now the child is being required to respond to what Father and Mother think is best for him, and not what he thinks (the issue of the will again).

It is not a basic need for a child to get what tastes good. Tastes fall into the area of wants—*not needs*. A young child can use dinner time to promote willfulness and manipulation (fathers are

Understanding Willfulness

sometimes better at sensing this than mothers), and these meal times offer daily opportunities for training in this area. When you sit down to eat, don't get into the habit of allowing your young children the freedom of "will" to choose the foods they do or do not want—you may begin to program a willful child. A child who eats as he chooses will probably develop other negatives as they grow older. Boys may develop a dislike for mowing the grass, or girls may develop a distaste for doing the dishes (just like they had a distaste for certain foods—even though those foods were good and wholesome and basic to a healthy diet).

Parents need to be discerning in what they are asking their children to eat, but if you know it is good for them, it is perfectly right to expect them to obey you in this area. I don't want to belabor this point, but it is important because food and taste likes and dislikes are related closely to fleshly demands; and when projected into the future of a child's life, these seemingly innocent "fleshly" desires and demands can get way out of hand.

Willfulness Projected into the Future

If parents are not sensitive to these so-called trivial situations of willfulness in a child, they are actually creating a willful pattern of life in this child that will need to be corrected at some point in the child's life and may still be present when this child reaches the teen years and adulthood. Keep in mind also that life in general will tend to not go well for this child because willfulness is actually a dishonoring attitude.

A child who contests or refuses the eating of certain foods or has some other seemingly trivial willful attitudes when certain situations or things don't suit their likes, will tend to challenge or refuse parental and Biblical (God's) standards in some areas of life as a teen or adult if they don't suit their likes. A child who eats as he chooses begins to reason that there are times when they can set their will over their parents', or that their judgment at times is on an equal basis with their parents'. Of course, this kind of reasoning when projected into the teen or adult years has a negative effect. They can reason there are certain times when they can act independently of God's will and not suffer for it, or they may think God sees morality as they see it (equal judgment).

Most significantly, these willful situations often cause the child to develop a disrespectful or dishonoring spirit or attitude towards the parent's wishes, and again they may have this same attitude towards Scripture or the will of God when older.

Parents should allow for different tastes or likes to some degree but the real issue to discern is the will. A child shouldn't be given a choice until they have reached an age when their choice can clearly be seen as one made with a subjective, respectful spirit.

Rewards for Obedience

Some parents, in an attempt to motivate their children towards obedience, offer some kind of temporal award system; this should be approached wisely and cautiously. It is good to encourage children in proper ways by expressing how pleased we have been with their conduct, and an unexpected gift or reward and words of praise will not only encourage them in their present conduct, but often motivates them towards desiring to do even better in other areas of their lives. "As a fining pot for silver, and the furnace for gold; so is a man to his praise." Prov. 27:21

Problems begin to arise when the child begins to perform only out of anticipation of such praise or rewards. They are becoming men pleasers. Problems also begin with children when they have begun to expect monetary payment for performing certain duties or responsibilities, whether these be domestic duties or spiritual responsibilities. Most children are, to some degree, selfish and self-centered—some more so, and some less. As the child approaches the teen years, this attitude seems to decline. However, if in those younger years, the child has been constantly motivated by some kind of self-gratifying reward or payment system, they will find it much more difficult to avoid this self-centered attitude as a teen and on into adulthood.

It would be better to bring home to your child a nice gift or take them out and buy something needful or useful for them than to give them a five dollar bill as a reward. Giving a child a gift that meets a basic need they may have steers them away from expecting something that may be self-gratifying or materialistic. In this way children learn that God supplies all the needs of those who are faithful to Him.

Those who are in Christian service are not to have desires towards filthy lucre or personal gain. We need to be careful we do not encourage these desires in our children by a money reward system. Be aware also that excessive honor or praise is similar to this. There are many today who have willingly exchanged or sacrificed financial gain for the satisfaction that comes with the praise and honor of men.

A child does not have to be very old to have a desire to please God and their parents (who represent the image of God to them). My children are easily motivated to righteous behavior when I express to them how they are or can become very pleasing to God by certain actions. Children usually delight to please their parents and God—that alone is generally sufficient motivation, and a child raised under this approach tends to transfer this desire to please over to a genuine desire to please God when older.

7

THE BEAUTY OF A SUBJECTIVE WILL

It is rather easy to see how important it is for a child to display a subjective will to his parents. A child who has learned to be subject to his parents' authority will, likewise, find it much easier when older to be subject to God's will and ministry for his or her life.

Jesus' life depicts this beautifully, and we read this account in Luke, Chapter 2, verses 41-51. When Jesus was twelve years old and onward, perhaps to the age of thirty when His ministry began, He is described as being "subject unto His parents." See Luke 2:51. During this period of His life, He was capable of living His life independently and gaining His guidance solely from God, the Father, but He chose to be subject to His parents.

Even at the age of thirty when His earthly ministry began, He still showed signs of this subjective attitude towards His mother's counsel. See John, Chapter 2. He voluntarily set His will under the will of His authorities. This is significant because we see that this same attitude was transferred to His relationship with God, the Father. We read these words which depict this attitude shortly before the crucifixion: "...nevertheless, not my will, but thine be done." Luke 22:42b

Those in Christian leadership described in I Tim. 3:4 were required to have their "...children in subjection with all gravity." In Titus 1:6, they were required to have "faithful children not accused of riot or unruly." This word unruly has in it the idea of having a subjective will.

Every child is different in this aspect of the will, and one of the most important skills a parent must gain in child training is how to control and shape the various, different wills of each of their children. The most effective way to gain and maintain this control of the will of your child is by beginning today, seeing to it that your child obeys you in all things with a respectful (honoring) attitude.

Gaining Your Child's Attention

A common problem I have heard expressed by parents is that their children will not listen to them. In an attempt to remedy this problem, some say that you should take the time to make eye contact with your child to be sure they are getting your instructions. This approach may have some merit; however, a child's failure to listen along with such things as forgetfulness are often signs that they really do not respect, value, or honor the parents' requests. If the child actually felt there was importance or value in what the parents were saying, they would listen and obey. So the real issue, here again, is the honoring spirit.

Granted, little children are forgetful, and sometimes a child's life can become so busy they do not listen to mother's or father's instructions. Sometimes parents can be part of the problem by asking too much of their child. But discerning parents need to differentiate between childish forgetfulness or inattentiveness and a dishonoring spirit that may be developing in the child. If the parent begins to sense it is the latter, it would be wise to reprove or use chastisement to help correct this willful, dishonoring spirit that is growing in the child—that it may be well with them. The child may need stronger measures to help them see the importance of respecting your wishes.

Be aware also that some children try to "look" right while at the same time are having an unsubjective will—this is the beginning of hypocrisy. This same child, upon reaching adulthood, may very well try to "look" right as a Christian (going through outward religious duties) but at the same time have an unwillingness to obey Scripture from the heart. This is why God urges parents to see that their child "honors" mother and father with their obedience.

It is essential that parents discern whether their child is displaying an honoring spirit or attitude when they are asked or required to obey them. Most parents can usually detect these wrong attitudes, and a dishonoring attitude in God's sight from a child is just as disobedient as defiance.

When you observe your child unwillingly or halfheartedly obeying you, then you know that they are not really respecting or honoring your requests and position of authority. If your child is allowed to do this consistently, you are teaching them that your counsel can be taken halfheartedly; and "...the eye that mocketh at his father and despiseth to obey his mother, the ravens of the valley shall pluck it out, and the young eagles shall eat it." Prov. 30:17 A child who is trained not to honor the value of his parents' instruction will eventually become blind to God's instruction and leading in his life.

Of course, children, like anyone else, are less likely to feel like honoring their parents if they sense an unloving attitude in the parents. But there is nothing wrong with parents telling their child that they do not like the attitude they are seeing displayed in their child. Actually, parents who do not take the time or effort to insist that their child obeys them with an honoring attitude are honoring their child above God; and this is exactly what God reproved Eli for—"...honourest thy sons above me...?" Samuel 2:29 Scripture (God's words) commands parents to see that their children obey them in all things; when we do not insist that our children do so, we, as Eli did, are honoring our child's will above God's will.

Disguised Disobedience

There have been times when our children have displayed disguised disobedience and then came up with the excuse, "I didn't think you would mind." However, they honestly didn't want to know for sure whether we minded or not, because they wanted to proceed with what they were doing. We usually told them that if they really wanted to do what was pleasing to Mom and Dad, then they would have wanted to ask first.

Be alert also to so-called "good deeds" of children which are done without first getting the OK or some kind of approval. This often is a sign of willfulness or independence of spirit.

For example, our children in their younger years were not allowed to go down to the barn unless they had been given permission and we knew where they were going to be. But one hot summer day, one of the children had noticed the sheep panting and ran down to put them into the barn. Upon their return to the house, they tried to make the excuse that they were very concerned for the sheep and wanted to help them by getting them in out of the sun; but, in reality, they should have and could have easily received permission first.

Remember, obedience is more important than sacrifice to God. "Hath the Lord as great delight in burnt offerings and sacrifices, as in obeying the voice of the Lord? Behold, to obey is better than sacrifice..." I Sam. 15:22   King Saul thought that his good work of offering a sacrifice would be pleasing to God; but he was rebuked for this and informed by Samuel that his obedience is what would have truly pleased God. Christians are admonished to maintain "good works", but no work or deed is good if it goes beyond God's approval, leading, or will. The same is true with our children.

The Will, the Spirit, and Spiritual Forces

The will of a child, and adults alike, is tied closely to the spirit of the individual. The common link that relates the will with the spirit is in the area of authority. Both good and evil spirits work through the structure of authority. If a child or a husband or wife are careful to keep themselves under their respective sources of authority (avoiding willfulness), they can expect to be protected spiritually.

When one is willfully disobedient to their authority, they have, in a spiritual sense, removed themselves and placed themselves out from under their authority's protective position over them. Willfulness, therefore, has much to say about the spiritual well-being of an individual. Defiance to or independence from God-ordained authority results in one being subject to or influenced by undesirable spiritual forces.

"Rebellion is as the sin of witchcraft." I Samuel 15:23 This Scripture suggests the presence of evil spiritual influence. Some have tried to teach that parents shouldn't restrain a child's will, claiming it will damage the child's spirit, but just the opposite is true.

There are times when we will recognize that there is spiritual evil operating in places of authority. "For we wrestle not against flesh and blood, but against...spiritual wickedness in high places (places of authority)." Eph. 6:12 So when we are in our proper place of subjection to our authorities, there will still always need to be the presence of wisdom to discern good from evil. But in a general sense, we are spiritually "protected" when we keep ourselves, or see to it that we keep those under our authority, in their proper place of subjection.

A willful or independent-minded child is one who is constantly challenging the right of the parent to be in a place of authority over them. They are thus more likely to be susceptible to these spiritual forces that can subtly influence them with wrong thoughts, actions, and behavior.

Creativity and the Will

As adults, we are instructed to bring every thought to the obedience of Christ. See II Cor. 10:5. Christ's will is directed to us through two major sources—one being the Word of God and the other, the Holy Spirit—and these two never contradict each other in our lives. When we as adults bring every thought to the subjection of Christ's authority over our lives, we are on the way to having a wise, discerning, spiritual life. When children learn to bring their thoughts to the obedience of their parents' will and instructions, they are learning the basis of bringing every thought to the obedience of Christ.

Bringing every thought within the bounds of our authority also promotes healthy creativity; however, when our creativity goes beyond the limits of our authorities' wishes, God's Word and the leadings of His Holy Spirit, then evil creativity and imagination begin to come forth. In Noah's day, God's spirit began to have to strive with man's spirit. Gen. 6:3   Evil creativity and imagination began to flourish, and men rebelled against their God-ordained authority. "And God saw that the wickedness of man was great in the earth, and that every imagination of the thoughts of his heart was only evil continually." Genesis 6:5

Exploration, imagination, and creativity begin to become evil when the respect for and submission to God-ordained authority is denied or circumvented in some way. This is why a willful child (and parent also) has the potential of coming up with some very wrong thinking. Creativity, imagination, and discovery can become evil if it is not restrained or channeled in proper, righteous, and wholesome ways.

We are not advocates of unguided exploration in children. When you swat a toddler's hands when they begin to discover electrical outlets or the stereo knobs, you are beginning to teach the importance of restrained exploration under the bounds of their authority. Unguided exploration of literature has similar effects. Allowing a child or young person to freely explore in a library or bookstore could be very detrimental, and the contents of home libraries should be carefully screened. Once a child's mind has been "enlightened" with an evil concept, Satan can much more readily tempt them with it.

8

THREE MAJOR AREAS OF CHILD BEHAVIOR INFLUENCE

When confronted with a behavior problem in a child, there are three major sources which may be found at the root of most problems:
1. The parents—Have we passed on or exemplified the wrong behavior to our child?
2. The child—Has the problem come from the inherent sin nature of the child?
3. Society (or his or her environment)—Has the child picked up wrong behavior from some kind of social or environmental influence?

The Parents

One evening my wife and I were attending an outreach program at a church we were attending. One woman was jokingly making this comment to a group of women my wife was with: "My husband told me he wanted me to wear a skirt tonight, but I told him if I couldn't wear the slacks I have on, I'm not going!"

Later that evening, we were back at the church for prayer after the outreach session. This same woman made a special prayer request of the group: "Would you all please pray for our teenage son? He has been very independent and rebellious lately, and we don't know quite how to handle him." Sadly, their child was beginning to display the same independent spirit that the mother did toward her husband.

Parents are never going to be perfect, but we need to realize that our children are going to pick up a lot from our example; so child training is also a parent training experience. The mother is particularly important as an example to her children in this area of the subjective will. In marriage, the wife's role is Biblically one of subjection. When the mother models the role of subjection in her home by being respectful and subject to her husband, the children much more readily grasp the importance of this in their own lives.

Parents need to present to their children by example how they, too, are seeking God's grace daily to make improvements in their own shortcomings. Children need to realize from the example of their parents that struggles with our old sin nature are a lifelong reality and a problem faced by children and adults alike. When children see this battle as a team effort where mom and dad are assisting them in finding answers to their struggles, they are far less likely to rebel.

Teen-agers especially like to see this team approach to victory. Teens often learn to discern the causes for their own struggles when we as parents willingly seek their counsel and comfort when we are feeling discouraged or have failed in some way ourselves. Confession of faults one to another and prayer for one another is a good practice around the home. Many times this is why children and teens seek companions outside the home in which they can confide; they are simply seeking understanding, comfort, and a team approach for the struggles they are facing in life. The rewards are immeasurable when they find this companionship and comfort with their own parents and a close brother or sister.

Don't let the world pressure you into thinking your child needs a best friend. Your home schooled child will have friendships, but when they have the comfort and security of a friendship with mother and father, they are far less likely to compromise with the friends they make. Indeed, our children greatly enjoy friendship with children who, like themselves, have found their bond at home to come first in their life.

However, it is difficult for children to feel this unity with mother and father when their parents are too preoccupied or overly involved with others. Christian service does require the giving of ourselves, but wives and children grow to resent husbands and fathers who are overly committed to others, yet have never given themselves at home first. God delights to see the dedication of a father and mother giving themselves in Christian service at home where there is little recognition and praise, for this is the real proof of one's sincerity.

To be the best example as a parent that we possibly can be to our children, we are required to grow in wisdom. Wisdom is basically the ability to discern good from evil. Wisdom requires discernment and judgment for every issue of life. "And this I pray that your love may abound yet more and more in knowledge and in all judgment; that ye may approve things that are excellent (or better)." Phil. 1:9,10

Just by taking the initiative to consider home schooling, you are trying to discern if this is something that is better for your child's life. Some try to make discerning parents out as "judgmental" when they attempt to make decisions concerning what is best for their child. They may even try to label you as rebellious if you challenge the way everybody else is doing things with their children. If you are vulnerable or persuaded by this adult "peer" pressure to conform to the way everybody else is raising their children, then consider how readily your child will fall for the peer pressure of the group you place them within. The world often tries to make us look foolish for even thinking we have a right or responsibility to train up our own children; they have falsely been persuaded that this is something we should delegate to others.

The Child's Sin Nature and Iniquities

We are all depraved and have inherited a fallen nature, children and adults alike, regardless of age. At the center of our depravity lies our willfulness, for whenever we yield to our old nature we are, in reality, in some way resisting God's righteous "will" for our lives. When we as parents help our child curb their willfulness through disciplinary measures, bringing their will into subjection to ours, we are teaching them a pattern which they will need to follow throughout life, for we also as adults are continually needing to curb our willfulness, bringing our way of life into conformity to the Scriptures.

Children commit specific sins like: willful defiance towards mom or dad, showing aggression or teasing towards brothers or sisters, being deceitful, selfish, arrogant, etc.; and each of these sins will require parents to take action to correct them.

Some sins can be corrected expediently, but parents will observe that there are other sins, sins which are more deeply rooted in the nature of the child, that are more difficult to correct. For example, back talk is easily recognized and can be rather quickly corrected by the consistent disciplining of the diligent parent. However, problems like stubbornness or independence are sometimes less recognizable and may take many months or even years to help your child correct or redirect these troublesome areas for more Godly purposes.

Take a problem like an independent nature in a given child; this has the potential of developing into rebelliousness if it isn't handled wisely. But, on the other hand, if this attitude is properly redirected for Godly purposes, the child can be encouraged to develop this attitude into the quality of "standing alone" or independently against evil, and standing alone for God's righteous ways is a quality much needed in our day.

Take the characteristic of stubbornness. If this tendency is not properly channeled, the child may tend to become defiant or unteachable. But if properly nurtured, the child can be encouraged to be steadfast (stubborn) about doing God's will and standing for the righteousness of the Word.

Even a child who is compliant by nature must be carefully trained and taught because a compliant child tends to be more adaptable, and we may find they are more willing to conform to or follow those who would lead them astray with wrong teaching.

Compliance, therefore, must be coupled with Biblical wisdom and discernment.

A prideful child can be trained to walk in integrity and truth rather than in self-righteous pride or self-confidence. David and Job both were accused of being proud, but, in reality, they were confident of the righteousness God had taught them and were walking in their integrity. Even a child who tends to lie more by nature can have this negative quality redirected for good purposes. Over a period of time, a child who is this way can be encouraged by the grace of God to be more truthful, and this same child will probably display a greater degree of tactfulness when older.

Many of the struggles our children face in their training are a product of this inherent sinful nature, and as parents we need to realize it will take time to redirect many of these negative qualities for Godly purposes.

Spiritual Birth

I have experienced constant struggle with my children in some areas of their behavior until they have come to Christ. Before their conversion, it seemed like it was mom and dad versus the sin nature of our child; but upon coming to Christ, there was the new power of the Holy Spirit working within creating righteousness in their lives. The presence of the Holy Spirit in their lives makes them much more willing to submit to God's righteous will.

We feel it is important to lead your child to Christ as early as possible, but they should not be urged to make an intellectual decision, nor an emotional one. Neither should they be compelled out of peer, sibling, or church group pressure. Observing parents who keep an intimate level of communication with their children will recognize when Christ is drawing the child to Himself; this would be the most appropriate time for that child's salvation experience. Pray with your child at this time or encourage your child to pray on their own asking Christ to come into their life and forgive their sins.

Even after coming to Christ, the child will show the presence of a sinful nature and the foolishness that accompanies this, and they will need the consistent and loving control of their parents to help them overcome their sinful tendencies. Even a saved child who is left to himself will bring his mother to shame. "The rod and reproof give wisdom, but a child left to himself bringeth his mother to shame." Prov. 29:15

Environmental Factors

We have found that the environment is probably the most important area to consider in molding the behavior of your child. Parental input is far less effective in a child's life if they are routinely placed in social situations where parental values are not reinforced or appreciated. In fact the child is actually encouraged by these situations to question the authority and value of their own parents.

Secondly, a child is less likely to make advancement towards conquering areas of their own sin nature if they are routinely placed in situations where these wrong actions are not exposed, rejected, and corrected. There is rarely a group schooling situation where this is consistently possible, due to the availability of companionships with other children who have similar sinful tendencies.

So by controlling the child's environment, we are creating an atmosphere where parental values can be respected and the child's sinful tendencies can be monitored and molded, making the environment the pivotal point upon which success in child rearing revolves.

This is why from the onset of this book, I have been discussing the effects of "evil communications" in child training. The environment at home thus needs to be wisely regulated, or those same stumbling blocks we are trying to avoid elsewhere will be brought in. It is good to get into the habit of spring cleaning possible sources of evil communication that may have crept into our lives and homes, and as we grow and mature spiritually, we will also become more sensitive and many times recognize the need to make changes in our child rearing practices and policies.

9

LEGALITY AND GRACE IN CHILD TRAINING

As I mentioned earlier, just requiring your child to obey you in "all things" is a giant step forward in creating a subjective will in your child, but with this one requirement, the conflict of the wills soon follows; and this is where much of the child training really begins. What are we to do as parents when our children either actively or passively reject or ignore what we request of them? What are the measures we need to take to see that our children obey our commands or requests? This will depend mostly upon the age of the child.

Two Phases in Child Training

We have observed two, basic training, time periods in the child training process concerning the will or obedience of our children. First, there is the "legal" phase which spreads from early toddler years to somewhere around the age of nine to twelve. This phase will require the setting of some rules and guidelines; the primary guideline is for children to "obey" their parents in all things. Certain punishments for violation of these legal requirements are also necessary.

Following this, say from the age of ten to thirteen or so to the age of twenty or thereabouts, children fall under the "grace" phase in training. In this phase, the child or teen will be inclined to obey out of a sense of conscience or inward desire to please God and their parents, rather than through legal requirements or rules, and punishment should be replaced with encouragement and counsel.

As parents, we need to approach our children with the proper response, either "legality" or "grace", depending on which method is appropriate for the age of the child. If a parent attempts to use the legal approach with a child of say fifteen years of age, this will tend to provoke rebellion from the child.

On the other hand, if parents of a young child, say six or seven, attempt to use the "grace" approach without legal requirements, they will also be encouraging rebellion from their child. Neither period of training is solely "legal" or "grace", but, in general, this is the way these periods are to be characterized.

During the "legal" phase, there will be much grace extended so that we can prepare our child to live under grace; likewise, during the "grace" period, there will be some legal requirements to keep the child from becoming careless with their freedom.

Bear in mind that the "law came by Moses" to prepare us today to live under the "grace and truth" brought in by Jesus Christ. "For the law was given by Moses, but grace and truth came by Jesus Christ." John 1:17   There needs to be a legal phase in child training to prepare the child for living the remainder of their life under grace and truth.

The Legal Phase

Someone might ask the question, "Why do we need to have a legal period of child training since we are now to live under grace and truth with the coming of Christ?" Similarly, we might ask, "Why do we need the Old Testament Scriptures then since we are living in the New Testament Age?"

The answer is simple—there is much written in the Old Testament to give us an understanding of God's requirements for our lives today and the consequences that come our way when these requirements are violated. They are examples (I Cor. 10:6) written for our admonition. The legal period of child training along with the appropriate consequences is God's way of training a child to understand the seriousness of taking lightly God's requirements for their lives.

As I have already said, there is basically one law that predominates during this legal phase—that children are to obey their parents in all things. Now there may be specific, stated things that children should obey, but there will also become a growing number of understood things that the child will need to obey.

For example, you might state to your child that they are not to go to the pond to check the ice alone without help from you, the parent, and you would thus expect their obedience. But it might be "understood", perhaps from past experience, that your children are not to "talk back" to mother and father disrespectfully—and thus their obedience is here again expected.

When a child violates one of these stated or understood requests, there needs to be an appropriate response by the parent to show there are consequences for misbehavior. Your child may need further *instructions* concerning what is expected of them; they may, however, have had sufficient instruction, and a stronger measure of *reproof* or even a *rebuke* may be necessary to affect the child to proper behavior. Finally, if these actions fail to produce a yielded "will" in your child, it may be necessary to take stronger steps yet and *correct* (spank) the child.

As adults, the Scriptures are given to us to bring about similar results in our obedience to God. "All Scripture is given by inspiration of God, and is profitable for doctrine, for reproof, for correction, for instruction in righteousness." II Tim. 3:16 Children in the early years of the legal phase (ages 3 or 4 to 6 or 7) usually do not respond consistently to instructions and reproof alone and thus occassionally require the use of correction or chastening.

In the Bible, the only method of correction for an unyielded child is the spanking (termed the use of the rod or switch). One does not find any evidence where a child was sent to their room, made to stand in the corner, yelled at, or deprived of a meal, etc., because most of these methods require somewhat of a rejecting attitude from the parents; and as I have said, rejection tends to damage the character and esteem of a child and subconsciously causes the child to reason that God pushes away or rejects those that have erred.

However, the correction of spanking can demonstrate to the child (if it is ministered in love) the parents' (and God's) displeasure with their actions, but at the same time their love and acceptance of them. In addition, the spanking does begin to instill in the child's mind the concept that there are definite consequences for violating God's laws and requirements for life.

It is not proper to use harsh and belittling words to affect a child to obedience; this also tends to attack the child's esteem and self-worth. Harsh words are usually employed when parents recognize that a rebuke isn't or hasn't been enough to correct the child, but neither is the parent willing to go to the needed, extra effort to spank the child. Granted, sometimes a child's disobedience does not seem to deserve a spanking, but it is better to lecture (a form of reproof) your child, trying to affect their conscience by pointing out their apparent guilt, than it is to use words of belittlement. If they appear to maintain a haughty or guiltless attitude about their misbehavior, then it probably would be best for the child to be spanked—preferably by the father.

Chapter 12 of Hebrews also indicates that God chastens and corrects adult Christians through scourging (literally spanking) in a similar way to how fathers were assumed to have corrected their children when those Scriptures were first written. "For whom the Lord loveth He chasteneth (corrects), and scourgeth every son whom He receiveth. If ye endure chastening, God dealeth with you as with sons; *for what son is he whom the father chasteneth not?*" Heb. 12:6,7

Proverbs 3, verses 11 and 12, indicate that spanking is a duty parents naturally accept when they "delight" in their children. "My son, despise not the chastening of the Lord; neither be weary of His correction: For whom the Lord loveth He correcteth; even as a father the son in whom he delighteth."

A Permissive Society

It is very likely that permissive societies are actually caused by an adult generation that was never corrected by reproof or spanking when they were children. There were rarely consequences for their wrong behavior as a child, so they have little fear of the consequences of their permissive behavior as adults.

Christians raised without reproof or spanking tend to feel as an adult that "all things are lawful" (See I Cor. 6:12), that they, too, can pretty well live according to what they feel is right in their own eyes and still receive God's praise and recognition when they reach heaven. In Deut. 12:8, we are told that "Ye shall not do after all the things that we do here this day, every man whatsoever is right in his own eyes."

We see that in the days of the Judges, however, that God's people did just that, and the days of the Judges were very corrupt days in the history of God's people. "Every man did that which was right in his own eyes." Judges 17:6 and 21:25 Similarly, in I Cor. 6:12 and 10:23, we are told that all things are lawful for us as Christians, but that all things are not expedient. There are things we can do lawfully because the law has been "taken out of the way" Col. 2:14c, but the results of these actions are not expedient or for our eventual good and edification.

Consistent disciplinary action by parents instills in a child from a young age this very thought that everything they choose to do may not be right—and it also may not be expedient for their life. This begins to place in their hearts the fear of God and the necessity in discerning the consequences of their actions in life; this is a very important ministry not only for your child's well-being but for the ultimate good of society and the glory of God.

10

THE ROD GIVES WISDOM

Through the legal stage in child training, spanking will be a necessary part of the training process. Today there is some debate as to whether spanking constitutes some form of child abuse, and unfortunately there may be some isolated situations where this has happened. But spanking, applied in Scriptural ways by a loving parent during these younger years, is in no way abusive and is laying the necessary ground work for shaping your child's behavior. "If ye endure chastening, God dealeth with you as with sons; for what son is he whom the father chasteneth not?" Hebrews 12:7

As stated in this Scripture, it is understood that fathers in the New Testament Age (today) are to use the spanking in disciplining their younger children. In the Proverbs, we have many examples as to what effect, both positive and negative if not used, that this kind of chastisement will have on the child. A discussion of some of these Proverbs and other related Scriptures may aid the parent in being able to wisely, lovingly, and graciously attend to this ministry.

Spanking is a Form of Love

According to Proverbs 13:24, a child who is not corrected with spanking may actually feel unloved and thus begin to excessively crave attention to fill this love gap, and sometimes this attention is achieved through misbehavior. This same child, when older, may also experience difficulty in understanding the love of God ("For whom the Lord *loveth* He chasteneth..." Heb. 12:6) and thus find it more difficult to come to Christ for salvation.

"He that spareth his rod hateth his son: but he that *loveth* him chasteneth him betimes (or early in life)." Prov. 13:24 Most adults who were spanked when little can look back with gratitude to their parents for taking *the time and effort* to help them overcome the struggles they faced with their own sin nature. They sensed, as this Proverb suggests, that someone loved them.

Don't let the world's methods lull you into thinking that this isn't necessary and valuable for your child's life. If you neglect this need to correct your child, they will subconsciously reason that you don't really care about them. He that spareth the rod is perceived as hating his son.

Granted, the rod or spanking must be ministered with graciousness, longsuffering, love, and discretion. A tyrannical use of spanking will certainly provoke a child to anger. This may also bring about a discouraged spirit in the child, and they may feel that it is hopeless to try to do what is right. "Fathers, provoke not your children to anger, lest they be discouraged." Col. 3:21 Be aware also, however, that some children try to put on a show of willful anger in a subtle effort to make parents *think* they are provoking them. Some particularly clever children know what they need to do to remain willful and to also keep their parents from attempting to correct them for it. "Chasten thy son while there is hope, and let not thy soul spare for his crying." Prov. 19:18

I recall a story of a mother who had spanked her child, but this child always retaliated with pouting and refusing to speak to the mother for several hours. This, along with such things as continued or excessive crying, verbal responses, threats, anger, or even delayed retaliation like doing something later in defiance are evidences that the child is far from obedience and perhaps even in a state of rebellion. What they are saying through these actions is this — "You can spank me this time, but if you do it again, this is what you're going to get! I'm going to make life miserable for you if you try to restrain me."

A child who responds this way is, of course, strong willed. I suggest confronting, or better yet, having the child's father confront the child by calmly saying, "I can see by your actions (or from what your mother has told me) that you do not really want to obey us in your heart which God would want; therefore, I am going to have to spank you *again.*" Remember, the subjective will is your objective, and it *will* come if you are persistent, even with stubborn children.

Spanking Didn't Work for Me

Some parents say, "I tried spanking and found it ineffective in changing my child's behavior." There may be several reasons why this seems to be the case:

1. Spanking will have little, lasting results in changing behavior if the misconduct is not *consistently* and *persistently* checked with reproof, instructions in righteousness, and correction (spanking). In order for us to have disciplined children, we will need to be disciplined in this responsibility of training them. It will inconvenience us at times to have to take the time to spank or instruct our child. But once a child has learned to readily respond to our first request or command, then we are avoiding a lot more inconvenience later. Neither is this a work left to the mother alone. This is very much the father's responsibility— "One that ruleth well *his* own house, having *his* children in subjection with all gravity." I Tim 3:4

It is best for the child to see father in this role of disciplining his children and instructing his children in righteous ways. At least half a dozen Proverbs address the parents *and specifically the fathers* with the importance of being responsible and diligent in correcting their children with the spanking and reproof. It must have been just as easy to neglect this work in those days as it is today, but just a little diligence on the parents' part in this area in those younger years of their children's lives will yield peace and fruitfulness in the years that follow.

2. Spanking will have less effect in making permanent changes in the child's behavior if the child is routinely placed in situations where this kind of wrong action is permitted, allowed, or encouraged. This, again, emphasizes the advantage of the home school environment, where behavior policies can be monitored.

3. The spanking will be less effective if the child has a companion or brother or sister who supports or at least doesn't question the wrong actions or attitude in the child that the parents are trying to correct. It may be necessary to separate your child from certain playmates or siblings for a while until you can be more confident that the negative behavior has subsided.

4. Finally, the spanking must incur sufficient discomfort to make the consequences of misbehavior more severe than the seemingly temporary rewards of willfulness and misbehavior. A spanking that doesn't smart a little will generally be ineffective and even teaches a child that God's corrections are inconsequential and God is thus not to be feared.

Spanking Removes Foolishness and Gives Wisdom

Proverbs 22:15 indicates that a child who is not spanked will retain foolishness in their heart. Foolishness is just the opposite of wisdom or just the opposite of God's ways; this same child when older may have difficulty discerning good from evil in their own lives as well as in others. "Foolishness is bound in the heart of a child; but the rod of correction shall drive it far from him." Prov. 22:15

Spanking Gives Life

According to Proverbs 23:13, a child who isn't corrected with spanking may meet with an early death or perhaps may not experience spiritual regeneration. This may be the result of the child not learning to "honor father and mother", and this "honoring" as noted earlier has with it a specific promise— "...that it may be well with thee, and thou mayest live long on the earth." "Withhold not discipline from the child; For if you strike and punish him with the [reedlike] rod, he will not die." Proverbs 23:13 Amplifed Bible

Spanking: An Inoculation

I like to compare the spanking of a child with inoculating them for certain diseases. Inoculations often cause a degree of trembling in a child's heart, and they do smart; but they are certainly profitable for the life and well-being of the child. I have never heard anyone describe an inoculation as "child abuse", even though they can be traumatic to a child. I remember sitting in the waiting room of our pediatrician's office watching a sobbing, little, three or four-year-old girl repeatedly saying for nearly an hour to her mother, "I don't want any of Dr. so and so." The child was there for vaccinations and a check-up and was terrified at the thought of getting a shot. But we know immunizations are for the good of our children (though they may seem unpleasant for the moment—like a spanking), and, therefore, we use them. "Now no chastening for the present seemeth to be joyous, but grievous: nevertheless, afterward it yieldeth the peaceable fruit of righteousness unto them which are exercised thereby." Hebrews 12:11

Spanking Prevents Shame

According to Proverbs 29:15, a child who isn't spanked and reproved will eventually bring shame to his mother and presumably to his entire household, and, therefore, also to the name of Christ and Christianity. "The rod and reproof give wisdom: but a child left to himself (undisciplined) bringeth his mother to shame." Prov. 29:15

Spanking Does Work

The spanking does work in changing behavior in the child

and for the good of the child. I remember my father telling me of a lifesaving incident with spanking that took place in my own childhood.

When I was around the age of four, we moved from the city to the country, and across the gravel road in front of our new house was a deep pond with steep sides. My father had told my sister (who was a little over a year older) and me not to go near the pond. One afternoon while playing in the front yard, our curiosity got the best of us, and we thought we would wander a little closer for just a peek at the forbidden zone.

Fortunately, my father was watching, so when we came close (neither of us could swim), he summoned us to come immediately to the garage (our wood shed). My father rarely spanked us, but we knew that he would if we disobeyed him. This was a critical situation, and it was certainly for our well-being and life that he impressed upon us the importance of obeying him with this issue. He told me that he spanked us both with a piece of wood shingle and that it scared us more than hurt us, but the sting was probably felt, too. He said that we never went near the pond again.

When Spanking Doesn't Work

This may sound strange, but there are times according to Prov. 22:8 when certain fathers have used spanking only to find their child to stray from upright ways when older. "He that soweth iniquity shall reap vanity: and the rod of his anger shall fail." Prov. 22:8

The cause of this lies to a large degree with the example we give to our children. Parents can be very strict and demanding with their children (this is what is meant by the phrase "the rod of his anger"), but if we are presenting a lifestyle or are sowing iniquity by the *example* we give to our child, even though we may not be aware of it, they will probably eventually follow our example to some degree, and the efforts we have made by spanking will only reap vanity or emptiness.

Every father or mother who is compelled to spank their child for certain misbehavior should afterwards stop and consider their own life to determine if they have the same or a similar fault in some form and then seek God's grace for self-improvement. Of course, this doesn't mean parents should be perfect before they discipline their child. We cannot use our own shortcomings as an excuse for not correcting our children; it is our God-given responsibility. But, we should be carefully considering similar faults in our own lives as well.

Spanking Prevents Tragedy

When my older boys were around six and nine, a very vivid and tragic example came along. I had been explaining to them how important it was to God that they obey their parents "in all things." They had been noticing some other boys who were very rebellious and unruly towards their Christian parents, and it didn't appear to my sons that those boys were suffering any ill effects for their disobedience. I assured my boys that those boys probably would if they didn't change, or if their parents didn't help them to change.

Then one afternoon shortly after this, a neighbor stopped by to meet me, as we were new in the area. My boys were with me in the front yard, and we got to talking about children. I asked him how many boys he had, but we didn't expect to hear the reply we received. He said, "I've got five boys, but really I had six....I killed one of them."

My sons began to seriously study the man's face as he explained what he meant. "Well, I didn't really kill him. It was an accident. My boys were all riding in my hay wagons, and I told them to all sit down inside and lean against the sides. I had this one son who never listened to me, and he got to sitting up on the front of the wagon and fell off between the wagons...."

Sure, God doesn't always come down on us immediately when we disobey a Biblical principle, but this event was not one to be easily forgotten for me or my sons; and I am sure God used this to impress upon my sons the truth of what I was teaching them about obeying their parents. I am also sure this poor father has many times since wished that he would have more vigorously required this lost son's obedience.

Don't Give Up

Proverbs 29:17 indicates that there are some youngsters who seem so willful and mischievous that frequent spankings may be necessary. God has graciously given those weary parents this Proverb to encourage them not to give up hope on this child. "Correct thy son, and he shall give thee rest; yea, he shall give delight unto thy soul." Prov. 29:17 We can only say this — Don't give up on such little blessings, for in time, if you faint not at setting your will over your child's will, they will begin to yield; and then you shall have "rest." Eventually through your labors, you shall see God and His grace turn this mischievous and willful zeal into a Godly zeal that will give "delight unto your soul."

God has designed little ones with a logical place where the rod (switch) is to be applied, where there is no risk of causing an injury. Do not use your hand or a heavy object, and if you do not have a switch at the moment, then perhaps it is a time to wait until you can find one.

When Jesus saw the money changers defiling the temple, He didn't rush in in a rage and start driving them out. The Scriptures very pointedly say that He sat down and made a whip and then, in a controlled frame of mind, drove them out.

It is important to have a controlled spirit in correcting a child. It doesn't hurt a child to have to think for a few minutes about the consequences of their misbehavior and pending punishment. As grown-ups, how often do we have to sit and ponder the results of our errors?

Someone may ask, "How strong do the spankings need to be?" Of course, this depends on the age, extent of willfulness, and gender of the child. Little girls do not need as severe a spanking as boys. Some children, particularly girls, will respond with a subjective will by merely a stern look or firm words. The important thing is to be *certain* your discipline is strong enough to promote a consistent, subjective will.

The Rod Gives Wisdom

The following is an excerpt from a booklet written by Al and Pat Fabrizio describing their experience with the early training of their youngest daughter.

There have been times when I have felt totally discouraged and defeated with my children until I had thought there was no hope, it's too late, I've lost so much ground that there is no recovery.

We went through a soul-wracking experience concerning our youngest daughter when she was around three years old. We were not being obedient to the Lord in her training. It was very involved and I am not sure how to explain it except to say we were relying on ourselves and on our own reasoning... in many instances rationalizing we did not need to spank her. In many ways we were afraid of her. We disciplined her just enough to maintain order but not training her to truly obey. We allowed her to maintain subtle control over us by attitudes of an unsubmitted will. We had a whole list of excuses why we were not obeying the Lord in this, but the Lord, in His grace, wouldn't give us peace. He brought us more and more under conviction about it until we were miserable.

*I kept telling the Lord, "I can't, I just can't do it." And He would answer, "I know you can't. Of course not, you never could." I would **say** "I can't" but kept struggling and trying. Finally I literally spent one entire night in tears telling the Lord that I was at the end of myself and if He wanted my children trained, He would have to do it.*

*The next morning, after a sleepless night, when the first occasion arose, I took the switch in hand and said, "Okay, Lord, You do it." And He did. Because I had trained my daughter to be **in**sensitive to my voice, I had to begin all over again to train her to listen. I spoke once and followed through with the switch. Each time as she sat on my lap and I loved and comforted her, I would repeat the words, "Listen to my voice and obey."*

At lunch time that day, after many incidents of correction, she sat down to eat and bowed her little head to pray and *thank the Lord for the food. Often before, she had prayed, "Lord, teach me to obey." But today she prayed, "Dear Lord, thank You that I **will** obey." She stressed the "will" as though she were saying, "Thank You, Lord, that Mommy is finally obeying You by making me obey. I'm so glad I am not left to myself."*

In the days that followed a beautiful transformation took place. She took on a new sparkle, became interested in others, and began to live outside herself. And what an inexpressible pleasure she became to her mommy and daddy and brothers and sister.[9]

Remember the importance of being consistent with your child through those times of reproof and correction. If your child requires a spanking, do so, and after the child has yielded their will and shown signs of repentence, put your arm around their shoulders, tell them you love them and God loves them, and then say, "Come on. Let's do something together." In this way, you're reassuring them that you're not rejecting them. They will not only sense a loving parent who cares enough to insist that their child obeys, but they will, above all, perceive the love of God towards those that are His.

---

*For those who have further concern in regards to this issue of spanking and child abuse, please see Addendum written by Pediatrician, Dr. James Sherman, page 163.

11

THE GRACE PHASE IN CHILD TRAINING

The second phase of child training is what I term the "grace" phase. Grace is a very real force or power for forming righteousness in the life of the believer. Grace is God's divine power which wrought our salvation and brings about the process of sanctification.

"According as His divine power (grace) hath given unto us all things that pertain unto life and godliness..." II Peter 1:3 From this phrase of Scripture, we see that grace first gives us *life* or salvation, and then it produces *Godliness* or sanctification in the Christian's life.

We are all constantly the recipients of God's grace, children and adults as well; and even in the "legal" phase of child training, God is continually extending this "divine power" (or grace) to our children. The rod and reproof are tools whereby we as parents are assisting the grace of God in helping our children in those younger years to gain progress over their sin nature.

In Galatians, the law or legality is described as a "schoolmaster" to bring us to Christ for His grace. One of the main themes of this letter to the Galatians centers around the futility in returning to legalism in gaining righteousness; they would "fall from grace" and "Christ would become of no effect unto them" in conquering their sin nature. See Gal. 5:4.

The same is true in child training; there needs to be a gradual phasing out of laws and regulations enforced by the rod and reproof as your child approaches the teen years. The "laws" will now be gradually replaced by "wisdom" in living righteously, and the punishment will be replaced by counseling and encouragement through the teen years of your child's life. "For the law was given by Moses, but grace and truth (wisdom) came by Jesus Christ." John 1:17

There is not a definite time when grace begins and legality ends. They tend to overlap, and some children require a longer legal phase than others; however, by the time a child reaches the teen years, they should be well into the grace phase, and this phase should be predominantly a wisdom training period of their life. It is that period when youth learn to foresee and avoid certain situations in life. "A prudent man foreseeth the evil, and hideth himself: but the simple pass on, and are punished." Prov. 22:3 and 27:12

Solomon wrote the first eight Proverbs to youth (perhaps his own children) with this very thought in mind of preparing them to foresee certain evil situations. In Proverbs, Chapter 1:8-19 and in Chapter 4:10-19, he stresses the importance of avoiding bad company. In Chapters 2:1-22, 5:1-23, 6:20-35, and 7:1-27, he exhorts youth to avoid certain situations which are immoral or that could arouse lust. Today this would also include refraining from certain social situations or literature that has emphasis on boy-girl passions, avoiding playing certain types of music or attending certain concerts, and avoiding work or training situations for youth which involve temptations or that may encourage a lifestyle that could create future discontentment with a family, home-oriented lifestyle in your child.

Proverbs 6:6-19 brings out the importance of teaching industriousness and responsibility to our youth while avoiding laziness. This would also include stressing the importance of orderliness and refraining from undue emphasis on needing to be constantly entertained or playing. Proverbs 6:1-5 points out the dangers of commitment to certain friendships or associations which may lead to the compromising of principles or Godly lifestyle.

Throughout this section of Proverbs, youth are, in numerous

places, being exhorted to draw from the counsel and instructions of their parents—particularly their fathers. "Hear, ye children, the instruction of a father," "My son, forget not my law," "Hear, O my son, and receive my sayings," etc.

This section of Proverbs is also full of admonition to seek wisdom above all things; parental counsel coupled with the pursuit of wisdom was to be paramount in the teen years.

The Need For Basic Discipline and Order

It is assumed, when I speak of deregulating the teen years of certain legal requirements, that your teen-ager has already acquired somewhat of a disciplined life through the legal phase in child training. However, if your teen-ager displays irresponsibility, sloppiness, or other undisciplined attitudes or mannerisms, then it may be necessary to try to establish some wholesome guidelines or requirements to prepare your child for a more orderly life. But here again, it is generally true that children who display such disorderly ways will probably have a parent who is likewise this way in some area of their life. So try the "team" approach with your teen. Confess your faults in the same area and work together for the same goals. You will be surprised at how much this encourages your young person.

Satan is the author of confusion, and he is constantly trying to promote this in all of our lives because he knows it will not only lead to disorderliness but it also eventually produces an undisciplined and unfruitful lifestyle.

He will use every imaginable means to bring about confusion. One of the favorite ways is to just get us too busy or involved. We all need to help and to be with others, but just getting too busy in this way will add a great deal of confusion and unfruitfulness to our lives. Husbands and wives need to discern their involvements together.

Getting rid of clutter around our homes, items seldom used, books, clothes, and items that bring up bad memories or that obligate us to others are among those that should be thrown away or given away to create more orderliness in our lives. Just by taking a few loads to the dump or a local thrift shop on a Saturday morning will help create orderliness and enhance our discernment while at the same time setting a good example for our children.

Grace Works From Within

Unlike the legal phase in which proper behavior in our children is created by some form of external requirement, reproof, or punishment, grace works within our hearts creating righteousness. For example, consider our salvation experience. Did someone force us to believe in Christ, or did we work for it? Of course not. God caused us to see and obey the truth by working within our hearts; the same is true in the grace phase of our Christian walk. There was probably some degree of desire or hunger for righteousness when coming to Christ, but it still had to be formed in our hearts by the grace of God.

This is why parental counsel and encouragement is important in the grace phase of child training, because encouragement creates desire or hunger in the heart of an individual which enables them to be open to the transforming power of grace. Motivating our children to the desire for righteousness by our example and encouragement should be a major part of teen-age child training.

The Elements Of Grace

As your child approaches the teen years, it is helpful to begin teaching them the different parts of grace so that they may more readily avail themselves to this transforming power. It has been our experience to observe some six basic elements or parts to grace; let me describe each of these parts in brief.

Part 1: The Goal Of Truth

The main goal of grace is to make us *doers* of the Word. "Be ye *doers* of the Word, and not hearers only, deceiving your own selves." James 1:22 The more Scripture we live and do, by the grace of God, the more we are transformed into the image of

Christ. Of course, the first Scriptures we must learn to do are those which speak in regards to salvation—the gospel of our salvation. "In whom ye also trusted, after that ye heard the word of truth, the gospel of your salvation..." Eph. 1:13a But following this experience, we then begin to come upon other Scripture for Christian living which we will need to do by the grace of God.

This is why it is important to teach little children to obey their parents "in all things," or to avoid evil company, or to keep their tongue, etc.—they are beginning to learn to be *doers* of the Word. Bible meditation, memorization, and application should be very much a part of child training with emphasis towards consistently doing the Scriptures—by the grace of God.

Part 2: In God's Timing

With this quest towards being a doer of the Word will come the obvious fact that it sometimes takes *time* to see the righteousness of certain Scripture formed in our lives. Time or waiting is very much a part of grace. There are so many verses admonishing us to wait patiently on the Lord, and parents need to keep this in mind when dealing with their teens in certain behavior areas. In this day of instant this or that, parents can sometimes grow impatient with their teen, particularly if they have encouraged them more than once in a given area; if the problem is deeply ingrained in your child's nature, it may take a more lengthy period of encouragement and counsel before a lasting victory is realized.

Isn't this true also for us adults, and don't we often have to *wait* for God to make changes in our lives? "We through the Spirit *wait* for the hope of righteousness by faith." Gal. 5:5 In reality, waiting on God to form the righteousness of truth in our hearts is an expression of our faith or confidence that He will do it in His timing—which brings us to this third element of grace—faith.

Part 3: Grace Involves Faith

"For by grace you have been saved through *faith*." Eph. 2:8a

Most every Christian recognizes the importance of faith and living a life of faith, but seldom do we recognize that God forms righteousness in our hearts by grace through faith after coming to Christ. For some reason, many believers realize they were saved by grace, but then they falsely begin to think they will perfect their shortcomings by human efforts or works. But, sanctification or the process of being made righteous or more holy is also only possible by grace through faith, not of works lest we should begin to boast.

This is a valuable truth for adults and teens alike. As your child approaches the teen years and on through to adulthood, encourage them to trust or have faith in God's divine power of grace to bring about victory in their lives. Encourage them to keep a diary of prayer and wisdom where they can record those areas in their life where they are seeking God's grace for victory, where they can keep an account of the spiritual truths God has taught them, and the little miracles He has done in their lives—this will greatly build their faith.

Part 4: Grace Through The Spirit

Grace is also operative *through the Spirit.* "We *through the Spirit* wait for the hope of righteousness by faith." Gal. 5:5 The presence and power of the Holy Spirit in our lives is that which raises us up above the sinful tendencies of our lives. "And what is the exceeding greatness of His power to us-ward who believe, according to the working of His mightly power, which He wrought in Christ when He raised Him from the dead..." Eph. 1:19 and 20

It is the Holy Spirit who is responsible for setting the circumstancs that led to our conversion. The Holy Spirit convicts individuals of their sinfulness, and He impresses upon us the righteousness of believing in Christ as Savior and also of the pending judgment that is ours if we neglect to repent and turn to Christ for salvation. "And when He (the Holy Spirit) is come, He will reprove the world of sin, and of righteousness, and of judgment." John 16:8

The Holy Spirit brought us to Christ for salvation, but He is also now a very important part of the process of sanctification in our lives. Learning to yield to the Holy Spirit's promptings in our lives is one of the most important aspects in viewing God's grace.

Take, for example, the Scripture, " Flee also youthful lusts." II Tim. 2:22a This is a directive for Christians that perhaps has particular emphasis for teens. God will be giving His grace in order to make your teen a doer of this Scripture; therefore, we should expect the Holy Spirit to prompt and lead us and our teens in such a way as to minimize the impact of these youthful passions until they have gained sufficient age and self-control to withstand such temptations.

When God brings along circumstances and situations which will help your teen avoid such youthful desires, make every effort to yield to the Spirit's leading in this. For example, if your teen falls ill or for some other reason cannot attend a certain event, see this as coming from the hand of God to perhaps help keep them from something that may not be that good for them. If your teen feels unskilled socially because of certain personality traits, see this also as something God has intended or allowed for your child. Encouraging social skills in your young person before they have grown sufficiently in Biblical wisdom and strength to withstand temptations may create a snare for their lives. The phrase "Flee also youthful lusts" is followed by the admonition to rather seek after "righteousness, faith, love, peace" and companionship with those who want "pureness in heart." See II Tim. 2:22 and I Tim. 6:11.

The Holy Spirit leads us in righteous and responsible Christian ways, but the Holy Spirit will not lead us to "work" in the energy of our flesh nor to follow the dictates of human intellect. Being "renewed in the spirit of our minds" (Eph. 4:23) requires us to mature in allowing the Holy Spirit to prompt and direct our thoughts.

Walking in the the "vanity of our minds" (Eph. 4:17) or to be carnally (natural or human) minded means that we are, in a sense, denying the Holy Spirit's guidance and choosing rather to make the smart or intelligent choices by human or worldly standards.

I urge parents not to try to make their children think they are smart or so-called intellectuals—they will only reap sad results from these worldly virtues. The Holy Spirit's leadings often seem unwise by worldly standards or viewpoint, but in time God will show you the fruit and blessedness in following His leadings. Academic skills can be mastered without undue emphasis on being, looking, or thinking we are smart. "The Lord knoweth the thoughts of the wise (smart by worldly standards), that they are vain." I Cor. 3:20

Part 5: Confession

A further important aspect to grace is *confession*. Consider your own salvation experience. Wasn't there the presence of acknowledging your sinfulness and seeking Christ's forgiveness? Confessing our own sin and shortcomings is essential in receiving grace to overcome sin. "He that covereth his sins shall not prosper, but whoso *confesseth* and forsaketh them shall have mercy (grace)." Prov. 28:13

Parents can teach their children at an early age the value of confession. When a young child has to be reprimanded (which may include spanking) for an offense, it is good practice every so often following such an episode to pray with your child, allowing them to confess their sins to Christ. Be specific. If your child has been corrected for "back talk," then have them acknowledge this specifically to God; this will be good conditioning for their lives.

When I was young, if I had offended a brother or sister or my mother by my misbehavior, my father would sometimes make me go to the one I had offended, confess my fault, and ask for their forgiveness. I remember having to go to my mother several times and tell her I was sorry, and she always forgave me when she knew I was sincere. This was a humbling experience and no doubt helped to prepare me to humble myself under the mighty hand of God when I was older and also had tremendous bearing on my future salvation experience.

This is something we have done from time to time in our own home, and this is also valuable training for preparing us to be willing to "confess our faults one to another" among Christian brothers and sisters in the church. James 5:16 Both humility and confession are essential parts of the Christian walk. "But He giveth more grace. Wherefore He saith, God resisteth the proud, but giveth grace unto the humble." James 4:6

Part 6: Wretchedness

There is one final element of grace which I call *wretchedness* or helplessness in our own ability to conquer sin. The Apostle Paul stated it this way: "O wretched man that I am! Who shall deliver me from this body of death?" Romans 7:24 God doesn't want us thinking it was our own efforts or good works that gave us this victory; this produces self-righteous pride. Salvation is "...the gift of God, not of works lest any man should boast." Eph. 2:9 Sanctification is the further working of this same gift of grace—not of works or human efforts.

From a very early age, as young as my children could comprehend it, I tried to explain to them that I didn't expect them to be righteous or have a goodness of their own. It is a big mistake to make your child think that he or she is "good," for they may fail to see the importance of being forgiven for their sinfulness and may falsely reason they have the capacity for being "good" on their own without the working of God's grace in their life.

Most everyone is annoyed by "do gooders." Praise for obedience is acceptable, whereas praise for being good tends to produce men-pleasers. David was praised by God because of his obedience "...I have found David, son of Jesse, a man after my own heart, who will *do* all my will." Acts 13:22 David was a God-pleaser.

In contrast, King Saul was a "good" boy when little and probably was often praised for being good. Saul, when older, carefully performed the religious rites and was one to dutifully offer a sacrifice, yet he was also frequently disobedient in his heart to God. It was more important to him what his peers thought of him rather than what God thought of him. Saul was a men-pleaser. See I Sam 13.

We have observed that often just prior to God giving us or our children victory over a sin or struggle, that we will find a flurry of wretchedness or sinfulness in that particular area. God often allows this in order for us to realize it was not our own human efforts or goodness that brought about success—but rather it was His grace alone.

Hindrances To Grace

"I do not frustrate the grace of God..." Gal. 2:21a There are several ways we can frustrate or hinder the power of grace and the victory it will bring in our lives as well as our children's. The following list may help us to be more aware of these subtle hindrances to God's grace:

The Will

Once when I was explaining the power of grace to a Christian brother, he remarked, "What if you don't want God to give you the victory over a sin? Can grace still be effective?" This question threw me for a while because I couldn't imagine somebody not wanting God to freely give them victory over a struggle or sin. But when you think about it, this is often the case.

I remember a couple of occasions several years before I was actually saved when men tried to share the gospel with me. I didn't want anything to do with it at that time, and I was perfectly content with my way of life. However, several weeks before the night that I came to Christ, I had a sudden change of heart about religious things and the Gospel...I was open to it! The grace of God does operate to change our desires and attitudes about righteous living—this is part of grace.

Granted, many times from a fleshly point of view, we don't really want to change (we [or our children] are enjoying what we [or they] are doing), but from a Biblical point of view, we may see that God would rather we (or they) change. We, as well as our children, need to be honest with ourselves and with God and tell the Lord that we need Him first to change our attitude about doing certain things. We need to ask Him to make us feel like doing what is right. He *can* make changes in our will. One definition of grace is: God giving us the *desire* and *ability* to do what is right.

Pride

Pride is probably one of the foremost ways we can short-circuit God's grace for our lives. Pride is often undetectable and subtle and can creep into our lives unnoticeably. For example, we can become proud by thinking home schoolers are better than others—by thinking we are attending the best church or are following the best Christian organization—or by thinking we are more zealous for God or are a harder worker than other Christians, etc.

You will notice in all of these examples that pride comes along when we are comparing ourselves in some way with others; comparison and competition are negative values. Avoid comparing your children with each other or others. It is helpful to encourage your child's self-worth and esteem and abilities, but be careful not to allow this praise to build pride or conceit in your child.

Legalism

There is not a law that can make us righteous; indeed, by the law we are made aware of our sinfulness. There is not a law that can take away sin; Christ and His grace must take them away. "The law was our school master (or training) to bring us unto Christ..."(Gal. 3:24) for His grace; there is, therefore, a usefulness in legality, particularly in training our young children before the age of 10-13. But during this legal stage, we should also constantly be pointing our children to grace. During the legal stage, try not to set too many strict or demanding laws. If your child knows how important it is to obey you "in all things," they will usually want to please you and avoid doing things that they are not certain are your will—even though you may not have set a rule or law for them to follow. It will bring you joy when your child comes and asks you about doing something when you have not set any rules for them to follow.

Put your teen in a position of choosing between right and wrong whenever possible, and try not to set too many rigid rules requiring their obedience. Grace worketh through love. In other words, we as adult Christians choose to do what is right because we know how much Christ loves us, and we want to please Him. The same is true in child training. When we set a lot of demanding regulations for their lives, we are, in effect, saying, "I don't trust you or your own decisions," and we will seem unloving to our child. Laws will not work as well as grace in teen training, and by allowing your child to choose between right and wrong by helping them to make wise decisions about their life, we are preparing them to live under grace.

It might be useful to point out that first born children usually have more of an ability to live under laws than say the second or third born. The nation of Israel was God's first born, and God soon placed the nation of Israel under His laws and statutes. The Church may be said to correspond more to God's second born, and the church is under grace and truth. The Church doesn't obey God's will out of legalism but rather through grace.

A first born child will much more readily respond to and obey laws. For this reason, parents will often falsely favor the older child because the older child seems to more easily fall in line with the regulations. When the second child comes along, this child will be less responsive to laws and rules and will want to know the truth or reasoning behind doing certain things (grace and truth), and often requires more grace to be obedient.

This sets up a good system. The second born will learn from the first born the value in following certain rules; but the first born will also learn from the second the importance in having reasons or truth for following the rules. They serve to compliment each other. Sibling rivalry which may grow into bitterness between first and second born can arise if the parents seem to show favoritism towards the older, more compliant-natured child. Actually, they are equally compliant; it is just that the second born requires more grace to comply. The second born often need more reassurance of loving acceptance and more of a friendship-encouragement relationship with dad (and mom)—they need to sense parental love and praise a little more, in general.

Some children, regardless of their birth order, seem to respond better to laws or rules than others. A child who needs more grace tends to seek out the wisdom (truth) behind doing certain things, whereas a child who readily responds to laws may not necessarily have to have a reason for their actions.

If you have teen-age children, begin today putting them under grace. Encourage them in their struggles. Point out the value of having faith in God's power of grace to help them gain victory. Talk to them about the time element, yielding to the Holy Spirit, and the dangers of pride and legalism (setting rules for themselves.) Grace is truly a light yoke to bear for adults and teens alike. Tell them that you don't expect them or yourself to have any righteous victories aside from God's grace. "Let us therefore come boldly unto the throne of grace, that we may obtain mercy, and find grace to help in time of need." Heb. 4:16

Dealing With Rebellious Teens With Grace

Perhaps you have been saved late in life or for some other reason have inadvertently come to have a rebellious or maybe just an uncooperative teen or young person in your home that has been making life seem difficult. What steps can be taken to reverse this negative situation? Many parents make the mistake of trying to tighten their grip on their teen or to aggressively criticize or condemn them for their apparent behavior.

Reheboam was facing rebellion and division with the nation of Israel upon the death of his father, Solomon. He falsely reasoned and also was falsely counseled to put a stronger, more demanding yoke (legalism) on the people to quell the revolt. But his demands actually led to further rebellion and to the eventual dividing of his kingdom. The most part of the nation forsook Reheboam and quickly found themselves in comradeship with Jeroboam, who led them into idolatry. Similarly, a strong hand towards teens can cause them to seek other companionship who will support or be more accepting of their views.

But something needs to be done. According to the Mosaic Law, parents are not to be held accountable for the sins of the children and vice versa, but not only the law but also many Proverbs and other Bible verses do indicate that it is a parental responsibility to train their children in proper ways. The problems parents face with teens are thus caused by both of these factors: the inherent sinful nature of the teen—*and* the failures of parents in child training. When parents try to place the blame solely on the child, they may have failed to wisely discern the complete cause of the problem.

So if problems have developed to some degree by both parents and child, it will require cooperation and confession on the part of both to begin to make a difference. Unfortunately, many of the shortcomings we see in our children are also present to some degree in our own lives as adults. This does have its good side though, because now as parents we can go to our teen and confess our shortcomings also in this same area, and our repentant attitude will help to encourage the same response in them.

If your teen has made some wrong companionships, look at your own life. Do you have some wrong affections in some ways too? If your teen feels comforted with worldly friends or ways, have you taken steps or sought God's help in keeping yourself from worldly associations at work? Do you condone the TV? Do you frequently associate with friends, acquaintances, or relatives who are worldly? Are there worldly magazines or books around your home? These are but a few of the areas in life that need to be considered as possible indicators to our children that we parents are, likewise, not heeding the admonition to be separate from the world. "Come out from among them (the world), and be ye separate, saith the Lord, and touch not the unclean thing (things the world readily accepts); and I will receive you." II Corinthians, 6:17 When your teen sees your boldness in standing against things of the world, they will be encouraged to follow your example.

If you have a teen who is beginning to drift away from the Lord and righteous living, I suggest going to them at a proper time. Be honest and open with them and try to accept most of the blame yourself for your child's behavior even though you know it may be largely their fault. You might say something like this: "Son (or Daughter), I think I have let you down by not being an encouragement and proper example to you of the Lord's ways in this area. I know you have been having your own struggles too, and I think a lot of the problem is my fault."

Be willing to bear the burden of your teen's faults and sins, and you will portray Christ's sacrifice to them. Most teens will be more than willing to accept their part of the problem and will either at that time or soon to follow express their own repentant desires. When they come to an agreement with you concerning the problem, take it a step further and seek their fellowship and cooperation in joining together in helping one another live a life more pleasing to the Lord. You will be surprised and delighted in the new friend you have gained.

If your child feels that you are "lording it" over them or have a "holier than thou" attitude, they will sense your pride and self-righteous attitude and will probably only respond with politeness—but still be unyielding in their heart to you. When you appear this way to your child, you become a "law" giver to them, and the law is very difficult to live under. However, when you seek to be their friend and acknowledge your own faults and shortcomings, they are placed under grace which is the best road to lasting success in the area of righteous living.

12

FAMILY BONDING

During the legal phase in child training and on into the grace phase, a family bond of unity and love should be built with each child, and this unity and love can be best established and nurtured through two main channels—communication and companionship/friendship. The disciples could sense Christ's great love for them through the communication He kept with them and the companionship He had with them. "Henceforth I call you not servants...but I have called you friends." John 15:15

At the same time, however, Jesus never compromised truth and righteousness with His disciples. Similarly, in order to build Godly family unity, it is essential that we as parents strive to build a companionship/friendship, love basis with our children while we also stand for the righteous judgment of God in their lives. It is important that there remain a balance of these two qualities for the child to gain a healthy and wise perception of God.

For example, if we become only companions with our child or so-to-speak "buddies" and neglect to set righteous standards and guidelines for them, they will begin to reason that they can do whatever they want and still command God's love. This is partly true; God does love us in spite of our sinfulness, but there are also definite, negative consequences when truth is violated. Children raised without restraint under a pacifist type of parental care tend to grow up to be permissive themselves and to promote this permissiveness in the lives of those for whom they become responsible.

It Takes Quantity Time To Build A Bond

It is surprising how few involvements it takes for parents to be robbed of the quantity time they need with their children on a daily basis. As my wife and I began turning our hearts more towards our marriage and family life, God began pruning back some of those other areas of Christian service that were bearing some fruit. "Every branch that beareth fruit, He purgeth (prunes) it, that it may bring forth more fruit." John 15:2 We soon began to see some better fruit right in our own home in our own children's lives.

A meaningful teaching relationship requires a degree of companionship and cooperation, so home schooling in itself tends to build a stronger parent-child bond. Working on family projects together further encourages these same qualities and will also teach children good working habits. The time to begin teaching your child disciplined work habits isn't when they reach adulthood. Begin early teaching them responsible work habits by such things as taking care of the animals together, working in the yard together, cleaning house together, grocery shopping together, etc.

The family bond grows even closer as you work on projects together. Our children fondly recall the barn we built, the antique sleigh we restored together, and the woodworking projects. As children work daily together alongside their parents, they will soon find it difficult to be idle with their free time and will use their time constructively. There are two important ingredients when teaching children industriousness—the first is quantity time spent together, and the second is being a good example to our children in this area of work habits. How can we expect our children to learn to be disciplined if we live an entertainment type lifestyle as adults?

Home Occupations And Home Industries Build Family Unity

The family-owned farm, business, or trade began to decline when the Industrial Revolution took place. The enticement of easy money and other temptations that were supposed to make life better began to erode away our nation's foundation that was built upon strong, unified families, homes, and farm life.

These big businesses and organizations made impressive claims as to the vast amounts of products they were producing. At the same time, the public school system began to acquire this production line approach to education. Christians also began to be attracted by this kind of philosophy, and the era of big, business-like churches and Christian organizations in America was started. Christian education has begun to follow along this same line of thinking. But all of this building of organizations, big businesses, and institutions has been done at the expense of the home.

I am very thankful that the Lord has enabled me to have and keep my home occupation, but when our children were young, I faced temptations to want to get involved and become part of a larger organization. They offered me things which I couldn't easily have as a small business owner like a guaranteed income, retirement, paid vacations, insurance, prestige, and even seeming opportunities to witness, etc.; but I had to make a decision as to which would come first in my life—my home or my career—and I have never regretted the decision I have made. Granted, it was difficult at first and took steps of faith and living daily by faith, but learning faith is also one of the added benefits of the family-owned business.

We realize that this may not be possible for all Christian fathers, and as Paul exhorts the Corinthians, "Let every man abide in the same calling wherein he was called." I Cor. 7:20 However, Paul continues to admonish Christian men and fathers in the verse that follows with, "Art thou called being a servant? Care not for it: *but if thou mayest be made free, use it rather."* I Cor. 7:21

There are few things that can build a family's unity and love among the members as much as working together. In operating my dental lab out of my home, my children have been able to help by starting early (at a young age) doing little jobs of responsibility. My daughters have helped with clerical tasks, and I have apprenticed my sons in the technical work.

In addition to academic studies, we have always felt that developing individual talents, interests, and skills is an essential part of a child's total education. Teaching children to be industrious and productive in "works for necessary uses" (Titus 3:14) not only enhances self-esteem and meets the need to prepare for the future, but also encourages the value in ministering to and meeting the needs of others. As our children matured, we began to recognize different interests and talents in each of their lives, and we tried to provide the proper Godly environment, the tools, and opportunities for them to develop these gifts from God.

Ben, our oldest, is twenty and has started his own dental lab along with mine. Ben laughs when he thinks of telling prospective customers that he now has over ten years of experience in the field. Ben has been blessed with being an exceptional craftsman, and around the age of fourteen, he came up with a new technique in the lab that saves several hours in production time each week.

Our seventeen-year-old son, Andy, has also mastered most of the lab skills and from a young age began displaying exceptional musical ability. He seems to prefer the classical guitar and plays worshipful melodies and hymns. When he was thirteen, he thought some guitar lessons might be helpful, but we wanted him to continue teaching himself, developing his own style. My wife taught Andy how to read music, and he took off from there. Andy recently produced his own cassette entitled, *Peace I Give Unto You*,[10] and now he's thankful that he can say he is mostly self-taught and can give the Lord the glory.

We're not saying that the Lord doesn't use other teachers, but are only trying to encourage Christian parents that so very much can not only be learned in the home—but will also be blessed. Today, we admire men and women *in history* who were self-taught, but so often we fail to see that this is still possible today. We underestimate the value of the character that is built and perfected in a child who is self-taught. Fanny Crosby (the famous hymn writer) was a self-taught poet. Thomas Edison was a self-taught inventor. Abraham Lincoln was a self-taught lawyer and politician. Charles Finney was a self-taught evangelist and preacher—to name only a few.

Joe, our thirteen-year-old son, has already learned many lab procedures, perhaps due to the advantage of having several instructors, and very much enjoys taking care of the family's large, but gentle draft horses and working with wood. He and Ben have each made several antique furniture reproductions which they sell at a nearby country store and are currently rebuilding an antique horse-drawn bobsled. In addition to this practical training my sons have gone through, they have developed a heart's desire for the Lord's work. "But ye know the proof of him, that, *as a son with his father,* he hath served with me in the Gospel." Phil. 2:22

My daughters, Charity and Bethany, have developed a similar industrious attitude working daily together with their mother in homemaking skills, menu and grocery planning and shopping together, cooking and baking together, sewing together, learning music together, and working on crafts and decorating together. Home skills are very fulfilling and rewarding and tend to make a young woman feel more home-oriented when older. Daughters best learn home management day by day at home working responsibly alongside their mother. A high school or college crash course on home economics will leave them poorly skilled in this area.

Both girls enjoy caring for their little flock of sheep and also help with our small, family-operated publishing company which we call *Parable Publishing House. Parable Publishing House* sprang out of our weekly, family story time. Years ago when we got rid of our TV, I began telling stories to the family as a form of entertainment and also to teach wholesome, family, Christian values like brotherly love, orderliness, respect, joyful family industry and unity, a Christian servant's spirit, faith, confidence that God controls and cares about everything in life, and many others. Our illustrated children's book, *A Thanksgiving Story in Vermont—1852*,[11] and story book, *Papa Leonardo*,[12] convey many of these values.

Finding Opportunities For Apprenticeship

Be alert and creative for apprenticeship opportunities that God will bring along for your sons. Of course, my sons have been blessed with the availability of my trade to learn, but they have also taken advantage of other opportunities that have come along. For example, through observing a furniture maker and by teaching themselves some skills in this field, they feel that they could develop their work with antique furniture reproductions into a profitable business.

My sons have often said that if they didn't have dental technology to learn, they would volunteer to work for free at a construction site or to assist some tradesman in some other field. The problem comes when young people think they have to be paid to work, but they seldom stop to think how expensive it is to pay for an education in school for some field or trade.

My sons have built board fence for neighbors, done painting, helped out on farms, driven heavy excavating equipment, and other things. We know of young home schooled boys who apprenticed under Godly men and have learned the plumbing trade, carpentry, automotive repair (mechanical and body work), art work and design, computer programming and other skills. I remember talking with a young man who was a partner in an electrical business. He said, "When all my buddies were out playing ball, I was running wire with my dad. They're still playing ball, but I've got my own business."

Steer your sons away from unskilled job opportunities (like sacking groceries). The income from these jobs will be of little value when compared to the time lost which could have been devoted to learning useful skills for their future. "And let ours also learn to maintain good works for necessary uses, that they be not unfruitful."   Titus 3:14

Building The Family Bond
Through Family Devotions And Family Bible Time

Family devotions should be the natural result of being a devoted family. The more that we as parents express the desire to live daily by faith, to live in appreciation of the works and will of God in our own lives and homes, and the more we demonstrate our desire to serve Christ by sharing the Gospel and Biblical truth with others, the more this will overflow into our children's lives.

On the other hand, if family devotions becomes a religious or mental exercise, it will have less value in shaping the attitude, faith, and spiritual well-being of our children. The more the Pharisees, Sadducees, and Herodians exercised their religious rites and mere intellectual study of Scripture, the more blinded they became to the simplicity in Christ and the life of faith that Jesus presented.

It does take a sense of discipline and responsibility in being in the Scriptures daily, meditating and memorizing, but be cautious of this becoming something done merely as a sense of religious duty. Religion and forms of religious activity have long been the greatest enemy to the true life of living by faith under God's grace, and we must be careful with this in our homes. It is important not to approach Bible study mentally or as just another academic subject (even though the Scriptures should be continually interwoven and applied to academic subjects). It should be a spiritual time, a special time, not a mere mental exercise. The family Bible time also plays an important part in the function of family counselor designated by the Scriptures to the parents.

We have found a relaxed, informal discussion of Scripture to be well received by our children. Even though we are speaking with our children throughout the day of how Scriptures apply to our lives, most days we have a more concentrated family devotion/discussion during our meals, and our conversations frequently center on Bible verses or passages we have individually read or memorized. It is encouraging for younger children to see father (or mother or an older brother or sister) describe how a particular Scripture has spoken to them or has had specific application to current life situations. In this way, we are demonstrating to our children how Scripture is to be lived and applied—and how we are to become "doers" of the Word and not mere "hearers" of it. We try to avoid structured devotions, although we usually find that several evenings a week, we may have a Bible study, Bible memory time, or Bible reading time together with the children taking turns reading before bed with discussion and prayer.

During times of family Bible teaching or discussion, it is important that wives honor their husband as spiritual teacher and leader, even if she thinks she has a better understanding of some truth. Children need to see her as the example to follow in honoring and respecting their father's leadership and oversight. It is also good for fathers to praise their wife in the presence of the children for certain spiritual insights and perceptions she has had from life or Scripture. This encourages the children to seek out similar spiritual concepts and applications from Scripture while bringing them at the same time through the discernment of their father.

Almost every night, when our children were quite young, my wife (or I) would rock them and sing Psalms, hymns, or spiritual songs to them, and as they grew older, we read a Bible story book to them before sleep. As our children began to read on their own, they continued reading through this same Bible story book. (We recommend *Egermeier's Bible Story Book.*)[13] They each read this book through several times and gradually, as they grew older, turned their interests to the Bible, itself.

Little children love to have someone read to them, and using this time before bed to instill this habit of Bible reading and reflection before sleep will not only wonderfully minister to the spiritual life of your child—but will also help to create a habit that will have a far reaching impact for the work of God's grace in their hearts.

When our oldest son was six or seven years old, he began reading his Bible in the evenings before falling asleep. He passed this practice on to his next younger brother, and they, in turn, also became an example to our three younger children. They have never grown tired of this, and they prefer to read their Bibles rather than other books at this special time they each have with the Lord before sleep.

Another tool God has greatly used in creating a strong family bond is daily communication. Almost every night before sleep, my wife and I individually have a time of talking with each of our children. We will share together our thoughts and feelings of the day's events, trying to comfort, guide, or encourage them through relating things to the Word.

Many nights, we have come away from these conversations with our children marveling at the encouragement they have been to us when they have shared their inner thoughts on the Bible passages and truths they have gained from their reading, meditating, or memory work. Through the years, my wife and I have tried to encourage our children spiritually. They have now copied our example and are becoming encouragers to us as well as to others.

The Special Dinner

As our children grew a little older, we began having a special family dinner on Saturday evenings. These were special spiritual times of communication when we would all get dressed up a little and eat in the dining room. (One house we lived in didn't have a dining room, so instead we set the kitchen table with the better dishes.)

Jesus communicated some of His deepest truths with His disciples over a special dinner—the last supper. As we began to use these special times, I would spend a few moments in preparation before dinner reading a passage or chapter in the Bible to teach and share with the family during our meal. Sometimes I read or discussed Scriptures that had been meaningful to me of late, and I often tried to personalize and apply verses to our daily life experiences.

We have tried to have a special dinner at least once a week, although occasionally we will miss a week in between. Our whole family has grown especially fond of these special times of spiritual uplift and have found them invaluable in ministering to our spirits and building a family, spiritual bond.

Sunday Evenings

One final activity that God has greatly used in our children's lives is recording their spiritual thoughts and insights in a family notebook. In addition to our special Saturday dinners, we usually find that our family has a special Bible sharing time on Sunday evenings.

To prepare for this our children will, sometime during the day on Sunday, write out a Bible teaching paper in which they express their thoughts on one or two related Bible passages. We feel this has been helpful in not only training our children to let the Lord guide them to meaningful passages for their daily life, but also helps them to express and communicate their thoughts on these Scriptures. These papers become a part of our family notebook.

Building a spiritual bond with our children requires playing and enjoying life together, working and learning together, and growing in spiritual truth and wisdom together. These ingredients will lead our children to a balanced lifestyle which will yield lasting fruit at home and outside the home.

Through the years we have had opportunities to meet many home schooling families and have observed a diversity of unique ministries for the Lord. It is our hope and prayer that other home schooling families will continue to use their home as a place of academics, home business and industry, and Christian ministry and worship.

13

MINISTERING TO THE SPIRIT OF YOUR CHILD

Many of the behavioral problems observed in young children and older children as well have their beginning with the lack of attention we as parents give to the spiritual influences on our children. In II Corinthians 7:1, we are admonished to cleanse ourselves from all filthiness of flesh and *spirit*. We wouldn't think of putting our children in an impure or immoral situation, but it is also needful that we take the time to consider and discern improper spiritual environments. Let us turn our attention to some of these sources of spiritual influence.

Music

One of the major sources of spiritual influence in all of our lives is music, and because it plays such an important part in our spiritual well-being, Satan is constantly at work in this area trying to desensitize our spirits to proper music. Our adversary will use music to create confusion, to lure us into roller coaster emotional swings, to create excitability, lusts, and even sensuality, etc.

Music in our modern times is having an even more significant impact on our spiritual well-being because it is readily available at our fingertips and is often piped into the work place. Constant daily exposure to various types of music (heard on the radio, tapes, etc.) often makes it difficult for us to distinguish between proper and improper music, and there is a broad spectrum of music types that lie somewhere in between.

We can even find ourselves becoming musically dependent (as is the case with those who are "hooked" on rock/rhythm type music—both Christian and secular) where an individual finds it difficult to enjoy the day without music to excite or move them. This young person (or even an adult) is in a precarious and defenseless situation where their joy and sustainment are not coming from a closeness with the Lord and His truth, but rather from hollow emotions and simplistic lyrics. Those who delight in this kind of music often are attracted to simplistic and emotional teachers who offer little, true substance for the Christian walk, and they sadly face the ultimate consequences of this approach to the Christian life. See Proverbs 1:20-33.

Even if music is properly soothing on our spirits and is melodious with a Godly message, if played at the wrong time it can create confusion and wrong emotions for the situation. "As he that taketh away a garment in cold weather, and as vinegar upon nitre, so is he that singeth songs to a heavy heart." Proverbs 25:20 Research has shown that infants who are placed in situations where wrong music is played will begin to acquire emotional patterns similar to that found in the music. They will learn to be up and down emotionally just like the music they are absorbing.

Home schooled children are less susceptible to the lure of so-called popular Christian music which is passed around and admired by social groups in schools, but keep in mind the potential of peer group influence found in church groups. These situations may also need to be wisely monitored.

In Ephesians, Chapter 5, where Paul is discussing the filling of the Holy Spirit, he there urges the Christian to maintain this spiritual state by singing Psalms and hymns in a melodious way unto the Lord. The melody coupled with Scripture is the ideal characteristic of music that will sustain a closeness in our hearts to Christ.

Years ago I began putting Psalms to melodies played on the

guitar, and I would sing these Psalms to my children before bed. The music not only relaxed and uplifted their hearts and spirits, but the messages contained in the Psalms often became the basis for many spiritual conversations. The one thing that makes the singing of Psalms so valuable is that we know that the message of those Scriptures is inspired or God breathed. We know there is a message there for us from God, and the wisdom gained will strengthen us.

Many hymns have Godly messages and proper melodies, but modern, popular, or contemporary type Christian music needs to be evaluated for its influence upon our spirits. Some claim that their Christian music doesn't have any heavy beat to it, but rhythmic beat or pulsating sounds are not always conveyed through bass notes. Some music is noticeably hyped-up, creating excitability which some Christians mistake for spirituality. Other types create just the opposite emotional swing. The up and down type of Christian, emotional life can sometimes be explained in part by the types of music to which we listen.

Try to evaluate the sources of musical intake for you and your children. If you are unable to sing Psalms or Godly hymns and spiritual songs to yourself, then carefully evaluate your music by the effect it has on your emotions and avoid emotional extremes as much as possible. Sometimes it is better to go with a few hours, or better yet a day, of silence to allow our emotions to settle and rest than to listen to music constantly. We don't need to listen to it as much as the world makes us think.

Finally do not let the world's philosophy trick you into thinking that youth have their types of music and adults have theirs. It is just another important part of our parental responsibility to realize this need to help our children to learn to wisely discern music quality just as they would a book or something similar. Parents usually have better discernment in this area, or at least they can have.

Playmates And Friends

A child will not only pick up wrong attitudes, thoughts, and actions from improper playmates and associations, but they will also unknowingly pick up the *spirit* of these influences. If you put your child consistently with a nervous, distracted, fidgety, or hyper child, you can expect your child to start becoming this way to some degree. If you allow your child to have constant contact with a stubborn, independent, or proud child, they will pick up these spiritual traits also.

Remember Eddie in *Leave It To Beaver*—how polite he was to Wally's parents, and yet his attitude and influence on Wally and Beaver were rarely positive? Look deeper into a playmate's or friend's behavior. There are many Christian children who are diligently instructed in politeness towards adults, yet they may not be that good of an example and a Godly spiritual influence for your child.

Prenatal Spiritual Ministry And Infant Bonding

Parents can begin to minister to the spirit of their child even before birth. An unborn child is perceptive to the emotional and spiritual contacts of its own mother. "And it came to pass, that, when Elisabeth heard the salutation of Mary, the babe leaped in her womb; and Elisabeth was filled with the Holy Spirit." Luke 1:41

Due to the sensitivity of an unborn child, we feel expecting mothers should limit their social involvements (hide themselves) and direct the emotional and spiritual environment of their homes with this in mind. "And after those days his wife Elisabeth conceived and hid herself five months..." Luke 1:24 A calm, contented baby can much more likely be expected if these measures of ministering to the spirit of your unborn child are taken into consideration. If you want your child to have good sleeping habits, then begin before birth with the mother getting proper sleep at night and a nap in the middle of the day if possible.

Avoid a hectic schedule, limit your social contact, have special dinners out with your husband, or have special dinners at home together centering your conversation around the Word of God and God's will and leading in your lives. As God gave us more babies, we began to have what our older children called "Late

Night Dinners." We would fix the children their dinner and, later on after the children were in bed, would have a quiet dinner together (although there were times when we would have a few, unexpected little guests.)

Seeing this unborn child, as well as your other children, as a special ministry from the Lord will encourage husbands and wives to evaluate the spiritual influences they are allowing to affect the expecting mother and the child she is carrying.

Even after the child is born and on into the toddler years, continue to evaluate the social involvements of both you and your child. Hannah would not go up to the temple with Samuel until he was weaned (she was deliberately limiting her social life). Hannah was intimately close and bonded with her child, and this gives us a clue to the reason for Samuel's closeness to God when older.

Babysitters

As parents, we can teach our young children to have a wise, discerning spirit even as infants. Wisely consider the spirit of your babysitter. Are they calm, using good judgment?

When our children were very young, the Lord brought to us an older Christian woman who had raised several children. She had never driven a car and always went places together with her husband, and she loved rocking our children and singing gentle Christian hymns to them.

When our children were a little older, God brought us another woman who had raised twelve children. She kept things in order, didn't try to "teach" our children her views, and spent most of her time knitting.

Grandparents can be good babysitters, provided they are in support of and are a strengthening to your principles and views on life and child rearing. At times, however, grandparents can *think* they know what's best for the grandchild and inadvertently or perhaps intentionally attempt to push their views off on the grandchildren. This can tend to be a source which causes conflicts between couples and rebellion in the children. For our children's sake, it is needful to choose a babysitter according to the proper spiritual influence they will have on the child rather than on family relationships.

It is best for your infant to get accustomed to the new babysitter before being left alone with them, and we feel it is also better if the babysitter can come to your own home if possible.

Even small children have a degree of sensitivity in evaluating the spirit of babysitters and social situations like nurseries. If your child cries or shows other apprehensions, then it may be wise to give some consideration to your child's spirit. They may sense something that you don't.

If your child has always seen you as faithful parents meeting their needs, the child will probably learn that they needn't question mommy or daddy's wishes to leave them in the care of a babysitter. Discerning parents will recognize if the child is using these crying episodes to manipulate or exert their will over their parents, or whether they justly feel insecure in a given situation.

My wife and I never felt quite right about putting our infants and toddlers in nursery care at church or other adult functions; it did not seem to be best for their spiritual and emotional well-being. Many parents pride themselves in how their children are totally secure when left alone in similar social situations like day care. These children are being taught some social adaptations which may have adverse affects and will also cause the child to not be naturally home oriented.

I recently heard a mother who is heavily dependent on child care for her children jokingly say, "My toddler would have little trouble making friends with any stranger on the street." The loose, social characteristic of a strange woman ("...her feet abide not in her house"—Proverbs 7:11b) and an immoral man are not only present when they reach adulthood but are beginning to be formed from a young age.

It is difficult even for the strongest of mothers to manage the household on her own. This is a responsibility to be shared between husband and wife. Wives do find short intervals of time away from their children with their husbands refreshing and spiritually strengthening, and they look forward to regular opportunities of communicating with their husband.

Many times wives feel they need a break from the children and justify a regular use of a babysitter because, due to lack of control and discipline problems, the children have been creating excessive stress on the mother. However, a situation like this is not greatly improved by trying to get away from it for awhile. These behavior problems need to be addressed by both parents together, and I would like to encourage fathers to take the responsibility of child discipline. Remember, fathers were to have *their* children in "control with all gravity." I Tim. 3:4 The husband is not the wife's helper in child training; this is an area where he should take the lead and responsibility.

As young teen-agers, my older sons were very capable of babysitting with our younger children if my wife and I wanted to be away for a short time together, but I don't believe I would give this responsibility to a daughter this age. My younger children use to remark how much better their older brother was at controlling things when we were gone for an hour or two than the babysitter (though she was an older lady who had raised children of her own).

The world sees nothing wrong with sending their young daughters to other homes for babysitting work. I think this is a mistake in judgment and puts daughters in awkward situations; it places them out from under their proper parental authority with its spiritual protection and discernment, and they may become subject to undesirable confrontation or influences. It also begins to train daughters to accept a false concept that they can properly function under or handle situations where they are alone or on their own.

It is very important to train daughters to have discretion and discernment in evaluating proper situations in life. We must not let the world dictate to us what is proper in these ways. The growing number of assaults we are hearing of today has to be correlated in a large degree to the socially accepted, independent lifestyle of the American woman. No matter how innocent the media tries to make this look, it is the result of women living in a non-Biblical lifestyle.

My fourteen-year-old daughter was recently talking with the wife of a professor at a Bible college. The woman made a comment something like this to my daughter: "I bet you are sure looking forward to getting your beginner's permit!"

When our daughter related the conversation later to her mother, she said, "I didn't really know what to say, Mom. I didn't want to sound rude or like I was rebuking her, but I felt like saying, 'No, not really'."

Our daughter went on to say that she hadn't even thought about driving because, truthfully, she wouldn't want to be alone driving anyhow, and whenever she did go anywhere, it was usually with her mother, brothers, or me.

We know of other home schooled young ladies who have a similar attitude and convictions about driving and being in other independent situations. I am not saying that Christian women should not drive, but that they should certainly use much more discretion with this and other practices than the world around us.

Improper Social Situations In Life

Today we are seeing an influx of teaching on the subject of bravery and courage for young girls. In some literature, a cautious (discreet) girl is made fun of for not having more courage, and we need to be aware of this subtle, false philosophy that is coming across. God often uses these feelings of caution or fear to alert daughters (and wives) to improper situations in life. Sometimes commonly accepted, social practices by the world around us can embolden daughters (and wives) in ways which are not really that good in God's sight.

Daughters need to be taught discretion so that they may wisely avoid certain situations in life. Among other Godly qualities in Titus 2:4 and 5, the older women (mothers) are urged to teach the younger women (probably through the teen years) discretion coupled with chaste reasoning. "That they may teach the young women to be sober, to love their husbands, to love their children, to be discreet, chaste, keepers at home..."

We realize that this is a very controversial subject and that there are widely differing opinions among home schoolers in regards to sending their young people to college, but we do not feel this is an ideal life situation especially for daughters. There may be some necessity for this with sons, particularly for trade schools, but we feel encouraging daughters to learn to function under such independent conditions is not best for their future. Many colleges are making correspondence study more available, and there is so much that can be learned at home or through apprentice type training under Godly people.

Much of the temptation that comes to sons and daughters in this area of the college social way of life is caused by them becoming discontent. Discontentment grows as they become more and more socially involved and socially dependent for their enjoyment in life. There are a lot of people who cannot enjoy themselves unless thay are busy with someone else.

The results of a recent national survey on the ten most pleasurable things in life in America revealed the social dependency of people today. The three top items each involved some kind of socialization—either socializing with relatives, friends, or other social situations. We need to realize that socializing is a very compelling pleasure in life, and sometimes the allurement of social pleasure is hidden in the guise of education or fellowship.

When social pleasure is coupled with a young person's thoughts towards finding a life partner, the college way of life becomes even more appealing. It would be wise to guide our young people away from such influences, for once a social, group-oriented way of life is acquired, it is difficult to once again turn a young person's heart to a home centered way of life.

Evaluating Literature And Recognizing Negative Programming

Go through your toddler's and preschooler's books—discerning those which have wholesome messages and pictures and discarding those that don't. As your child gets older, begin to discern together the examples that are presented in materials, helping them to see the things that are good and the things that are not so good which could be a temptation to them and present ungodly ways. This will begin to instill in this child a discerning spirit of wisdom for the future when similar decisions will constantly need to be made.

"Be not thou envious of evil men, neither desire to be with them." Proverbs 24:1 Evil men are not only presented to us though socialization but also, in a very real sense, through literature. Think of the Bible stories, "The Rich Man and Lazarus" or "The Prodigal Son." When we read these stories that Jesus told, don't the people seem like real individuals to us? In the same way, animated characters and other types of make-believe seem very real to our children. Many forms of evil can be presented to children on their level through cartoons. "Goofy" is just who he says he is, and he promotes an uncontrolled spirit of silliness and goofiness to children. Children can have fun without excessiveness in this area. "Foolishness is bound up in the heart of a child."...Prov. 22:15 There's no sense in encouraging it further with comics or cartoons.

These cartoon characters may appear harmless, but they are not; and be careful also with animated and other similar type stories that subtly present negative qualities like:

complaining—which opposes meekness and being thankful in all things

frightening situations or pictures—which opposes realizing that God controls all things

disrespectful attitudes or sarcasm—which opposes faith and understanding that God works through authority

independent attitudes and actions—which places us out from under proper, spiritual protection

being smart—which opposes learning to live in God's Spirit and taking steps of faith which do not always appear as the smart thing to do

unkind words or actions—which oppose love, longsuffering, mercy, and giving of ourselves

unbelief, pride, foolishness—which oppose faith, confidence in God only, and Biblical wisdom

Ministering to the Spirit of Your Child

Many times when there is an attempt to present good qualities in children's literature, evil is being subtly mixed in and presented along with it. One good point was crowded in with some evil. This literature then, rather than causing positive virtues, will actually arouse wrong ideas and thinking in children's minds. This is what I call negative programming.

In Romans 16:19c, Paul exhorts, "But yet I would have you wise unto that which is good, *and simple concerning evil.*" To be simple is to be unknowledgeable or ignorant. It is a positive quality to be a simpleton concerning evil, and it is good not to even allow this evil to enter the minds of our children.

"For it is a shame (too shameful) even to speak of those things which are done of them in secret." Ephesians 5:12 Sometimes you will hear well-intentioned preaching and teaching on evil or immoral subjects, but I think it would be better not to even speak of these sins of the world; it only puts the knowledge of wrong thinking into the audience's minds. (See Philippians 4:8.) It also makes this kind of talk commonplace, and thus our consciences become desensitized in this area. Remember the example of the woman at the well when she met Jesus and believed in Him. Later when giving her testimony, she didn't go into a lengthy or vividly descriptive narrative of the sins she had committed, but simply shared, "Come see a man, which told me all things that ever I did: is not this the Christ?" John 4:29

Much of what is in the news media today, especially photography as seen in the newspaper and on TV, is impure and immoral and can easily cause fear and wrong thinking in a young person's mind. I have observed that my wife and daughters seem to become more alarmed and troubled in spirit with the content of news heard on the radio or read in a newspaper, and news events seem to cause greater fear in their lives than they do in myself or in my sons. For this reason, we do not take a daily newspaper, and either I or one of my older sons (when they have reached the age of having wisdom and discernment) usually relate to the family those news items which are of value or relevance to our lives. News events and newscasters can tend to cause us to feel insecure and that God isn't in control of things in the world—which He very much is.

Be cautious with some so-called character building correspondence (through books, children's videos, etc.) which shroud one positive concept or example amongst some negative ones. For example, a Christian friend of ours was sharing about some character building story tapes they had ordered for their children. One of the first tapes was supposed to present the quality of thankfulness, but our friend said, "Oh sure, at the end of the story, they were thankful; but until the end, there was so much sarcasm and disrespectful talk. I'm afraid that's about all my kids picked up out of the story."

One of my sons was telling me about a similar so-called character story he had listened to on the radio. The concept that was supposed to be presented in the story was patience, but a young teen-age boy riding in the car with his father kept trying to persuade his father to let him drive. The father tried to patiently explain that the boy wasn't old enough yet and needed to be patient. The son complained, argued, and said things like, "All the other boys at school get to drive before they're old enough," and, in general, made his father out to be unreasonable....but finally at the end of the conversation, the boy halfheartedley admitted he needed patience. My son said, "Most young people listening to this story will much more readily imitate the negative attitude, sarcasm, and disrespect this boy had towards his father and the government—his indifference towards honesty—and the way the teen-age boy was influenced by the practices of his peers—rather than the character quality of patience."

Another Christian home schooling friend of ours was describing things like witchcraft, sorcery, wizardry, fairy tales, and other negative influences she was finding in so-called Christian literature. She made the statement, "If my children are going to have holes in their literary education, then they're just going to have to have holes in it, because I'm not going to let them read that stuff." She did realize, however, that she was not really creating holes in her children's education from a Christian perspective; this mother was wisely guarding her children's minds from certain intake.

Some materials set Bible stories in context with fairy tales. On one page you may find a Bible passage used as an example and on the opposite page a fairy tale or fantasy. In a child's mind, these are presented on an equal basis, and this confuses their discernment. Jesus taught in parables, which was a form of Godly fiction, presenting real truth in the framework of a story which could be easily related to and applied to everyday life.

Many people erroneously think, however, that fairy tales, fantasy fiction, fables, and myths are designed to present useful moral teaching or other wholesome values, but, in general, they do not. Attention to fables is warned against five times in the New Testament because they tend to liberalize true, Biblical, moral values and thinking. We suggest passing over these worldly forms of material altogether when your children are younger, and when they are older, point out to your child why these kinds of stories are not good or edifying to their lives.

Be alert also to less obvious wrong. Watch out for stories that emphasize pride in self, self-confidence, self-guidance in children, independence in girls and women, mind or intellect exalting philosophies, and envying and striving (which is competitiveness), etc.

Some materials try to encourage mothers to teach their children every sort of meaningless and useless knowledge: things like teaching your kids to dance an Indian dance, or to talk or walk like a cowboy, or other similar foolish things. If you are going to teach your children these kinds of vain things, then you might as well have them mimic every example they see on the street or notice in the neighborhood. Instead, teach your child to have wise, sober, and Godly discernment, and to turn away from such things.

Creating A Peaceful And Spiritual Environment

There is much to be said of the country way of life for ministering to the spirits of our children. People have often remarked at how calm our children are, but years ago we began to become more nature, farm, and country-oriented—and we are surprised at how sensitive our children's spirits are to the Holy Spirit's promptings and leadings, and how quickly they identify negative, spiritual influence.

We began substituting taking care of domestic animals for heavy involvement in sports. One time while cleaning up our small barn together, we were joyfully discussing all the positive character qualities that taking care of domestic animals produces.

First, there's just something spiritual and peaceful about an orderly barn. (It was no mistake that Jesus was born in a stable.) There is the need for a calm, gentle, but firm spirit in handling animals like horses and sheep. There's the need for dependability, responsibility, compassion, patience, protectiveness, a servant's spirit, tolerance, and others.

Actually, these same qualities are needed in child training and are also valuable to have in Christian leadership. Children can learn through experience these basic character qualities by first learning to take care of dogs, sheep, goats, horses, ponies, chickens, and ducks, etc.

The family garden which most every family kept up until recent years offers additional opportunity to learn qualities like patience, planning ahead, neatness and orderliness, faith, hope, and dependence on God's blessing, etc.

A family doesn't really need a lot of acreage to have this kind of environment. We once lived in a home on three acres of woods in the country and found it very spiritually rewarding while we daily marveled over God's creation around us. Many great men of the Bible were men who lived a large part of their lives with nature and caring for domestic animals. Moses and David were shepherds, and Elisha was a farmer. Elijah, John the Baptist, and Jesus spent much time in wilderness places. These men each possessed sensitive, discerning spirits, and their nature-oriented lifestyle played an important part in promoting this.

Spiritual Values In Orderliness

Start at a young age encouraging your children with orderliness and neatness. Children will learn this best as you work alongside

Ministering to the Spirit of Your Child

them in forming these habits. Disorder (or confusion) is one of the greatest hindrances there is to discerning the leading and will of God as revealed to us by the Holy Spirit and the Word of God. If we allow our child's life to be disorderly, confusing, and in other ways distracting, their spiritual discernment will be proportionally weak.

Many Christian wives have erroneously come to the conclusion that they are in some way serving Christ in their home by picking up after and dutifully serving the whims and demands of their children. But may I remind you that the virtuous woman in Proverbs 31 and I Tim. 5:14 "guided the affairs of her home" — she had somewhat of a managerial role in the affairs of the household.

Many women today are tricked into thinking they are virtuous by being the household slave when, in reality, responsibility should be shared and delegated to those suitably capable. Neither do we feel the other extreme is proper either where children are paid or hired to do routine, household responsibilities. They are not our slaves either. But rather these responsibilities should be shared and attended to together as a family with a spirit of consideration and cooperation.

We did not teach our children to thank their mother for cleaning up their room or for making their bed, but taught them to keep their own room orderly and neat. It was something we expected of them, and once they developed a responsible attitude about it, they not only willingly accepted this task, but orderliness soon became a part of their daily routine. Housekeeping and other more major cleaning needs were something we worked together on, and even our sons helped out responsibly with this (we felt this would give them necessary training for their future lives—whether single or married).

My daughters could clean the whole house, prepare a complete dinner, and do the ironing, laundry and mending by the age of ten to twelve. My sons also by this age could clean the house and responsibly see the need to straighten up the garage or basement and take care of the mowing needs without being told.

By the age of sixteen or seventeen, my sons could efficiently and skillfully run my dental lab in my absence. Many people think Benjamin Franklin was such a genius for operating a print shop as a young teen-ager, but, in reality, he was really just a typically responsible young man of his day. Now the world is deceived into thinking this is not possible until college graduation.

Actually, orderliness is one of the most valuable traits we can teach our children because it provides basic training in spiritual discernment. Wisdom is the ability to discern between good and evil for our lives—this is spiritual discernment. Solomon asked for wisdom that he might be able to "discern good from bad." I Kings 3:9

When you teach your child to get rid of clutter or to throw away useless things, they are learning to discern what is valuable and useful for their lives and what is not. When you teach your children to pick out clothing with color combinations that are coordinated and orderly, they are developing and using a degree of spiritual discernment. When you teach a child to put things in order or to straighten a drawer, they are learning the quality of organizing their thoughts about life in general. They will gain a similar orderly attitude about spiritual truth. They will learn to discard or reject concepts that are not good for their lives, and they will learn to adopt and put into practice those which are good. Orderliness promotes spiritual discernment which will help lead your child on the pathway to wisdom.

14

FURTHER SPIRITUAL TRAINING

There are many factors which play a part in the spiritual well-being of not only our children, individually, but also in our family life in general. If we fail to give sufficient attention to these factors, we can become discouraged with the spiritual quality of our home life. Husbands, wives, and children also may become discontent with each other and with staying at home, and this eventually results in the family becoming socially dependent for their enjoyment in life. Let us turn our attention to some of these further spiritual conditions in the home.

Disruptive Behavior

On occasion, parents may find the orderliness of their day and the spiritual tranquility of their home to be disrupted by a child who displays such negative behavioral qualities as hyperactivity, excessive willfulness, attention deficiencies, or other seemingly uncontrollable mannerisms. The first step in correcting such problems is to recognize that there are three probable major sources for causing these conditions.

1. The Child

The problem has its beginning in the nature of the child himself or herself. The child may be more active or have more energy than usual—or may tend to be more willful or stubborn by nature—or may have a tendency to be more easily distracted. However, these qualities in themselves are not necessarily that negative. For example, a child who has more energy than others can have this energy channelled into making this child an energetic servant for Christ and Godly purposes. But on the other hand, if this energy is not properly handled, the child may become hyperactive in getting into mischief or becoming overly nervous and demanding, etc.

The strong-willed or stubborn child can have this re-directed for the good by making him or her steadfast or stubborn about righteousness. However, if the child is left to himself or herself with this problem and is not properly guided and trained by the parents, the child may become unrulable. So this brings us to the second important factor in shaping the disruptive child.

2. The Parents

The earlier that the parents can recognize and begin to work on the oncoming behavioral conflicts with a child who begins to show one of these behavioral extremes, the more easily success is achieved. But it will require diligence and discipline on the part of the parent. It is often the child who has an extreme behavioral tendency who also has the potential for eventually becoming very useful and productive for the Lord.

Parents who are not willing to put the effort into shaping such a child often try to place all the blame on the child or make excuses for having an uncontrollable child. They will make comments like, "He just has so much more energy than my other children did" or "I've done fine with my other children, but this one is something else." These excuses should not be used as reasons why the parents can't have control, but should serve as signals that they will need a more concentrated effort to gain and maintain control. The father will probably need to be more active in helping to shape the behavior of this child.

3. The Environment

Finally do not neglect attention given to this child's environment. For example, grandparents or baby-sitters can tolerate an extremely disruptive child because they are only with the child two or three hours at a time or maybe a few days. Then it's all over, and they can recuperate; but the parents and brothers and sisters have to live with this unpleasant behavior daily, and the parents will eventually have to shoulder much of the ridicule for this child who will probably "bringeth his mother to shame." Prov. 29:15 So try to encourage the cooperation of grandparents and baby-sitters in dealing with children who display these excessive traits. If the child doesn't have a place where they can go and act out mischievously this way, the condition will have a tendency to subside. Sometimes grandparents, playmates, acquaintances, and friends can actually inadvertently encourage these negative ways in your child.

Hyperactivity

Varying levels of hyperactivity in just one child in a family can make life stressful and disheartening for all. The hyperactive child tends to have a lot of energy, emotions, and independence, and is usually very inquisitive and curious by nature. However, as we just said, these are not necessarily negative qualities. They simply are going to require more diligence and intense child training with a greater degree of restraint, guidance, and channeling.

Try to begin early in helping your child learn to subject his will to yours. Hyperactivity is very much a situation caused by the child's lack of self-control, and the hyperactive child will need assistance from their parents in gaining this self-control. Have them learn to sit quietly for a period of time and to learn to be quieter and not ask too many questions. Remember, the tongue has a lot to do with controlling our whole bodies. See James, Chapter 3.

Don't allow this child to be manipulative, assertive, or demanding—these are actually signs of willfulness. In many cases of hyperactive children, the parents are unaware that the child has control over the parents, rather than the parents having control over their children. Often parents try to place the blame for hyperactivity on such things as genetic inheritance, hormone imbalances, and the individual child's unique personality, etc. These may be contributing factors, but they may be only part of the problem.

Another important factor which can bring about or intensify the condition of hyperactivity is the environment and excessive social contacts. Carefully regulate and be mindful of environmental situations which might tip these tendencies observed in your child into the hyper range. Here again, go through the list of possible sources: excited and overly emotional friends, relatives, and acquaintances who are not good behavioral examples for your child, excited or dramatic speakers or teachers, literature, videos, TV, hyped-up music, and other mediums that may encourage this condition. Also, carefully evaluate the atmosphere at home; disorderliness and confusion tend to add to the problem.

Attention deficiencies and hyperactivity are more prevalent in group schooled children or in children who are in constant social contact than with those taught at home where the spirit of the home environment can be controlled. Unfortunately, however, these same problems can surface in home schooled children as well.

One home schooling mother was sadly relating the hyperactivity she was trying to control in her son. Of course, she was following the normal treatment procedures of diet and drugs, but we could see a major cause of the problem rather easily.

The mother was living a very busy and distracted lifestyle herself, and she was always "on the go." There was little orderliness to her housekeeping or daily schedule, and her school program was confusing, stressful, and extremely demanding. The family was overly involved, and the mother was constantly reading every "wind of doctrine" (Eph. 4:14) that came along. Furthermore, her music likes were fast paced and emotional. This mother's lifestyle and spirit were perfectly portrayed in her son with whom she was so aggravated.

Many times the parents themselves are overly active (hyper) but in ways which do not appear so offensive; however, the child can become a mirror of many of these ways with attitudes and behavior which are offensive. Parents with so-called hyperactive children or other supposedly extreme behavioral disorders would be wise to first take steps to evaluate and control these areas of child behavior influence before seeking medical assistance for these problems.

Spiritual Awakening

Around the age of twelve as a young person moves more into the period of grace in their training, they should be observed to show increasing signs of spiritual interest and insight, provided they have already experienced salvation. They may be seen to more often draw certain applications, teachings, or observations from the Scriptures for life in general. The age of twelve or thereabouts should mark the beginning of a new spiritual awareness that will continue throughout life.

It was at the age of twelve that Jesus began to be "about His Father's business" (Luke 2:49), and it was also at this age that Jesus began to show His spiritual insight to the doctors in the temple. This is not to say that some children younger than twelve will not display certain spiritual abilities, but that, in general, there begins to be a shift from dependence on dad and mom's instructions and Biblical teaching to drawing certain truth and insights of their own from the Word and from God, Himself. In a sense, they too begin to be more about their heavenly Father's business as well. Encourage your child with their spiritual reasoning as much as possible during this period of their life. This will greatly add to the spiritual quality of your home life.

This spiritual awakening comes at a very important time in the young person's life, because it is also around this time that compelling physical desires begin to develop which must be brought under control. In Galatians 5:17, we read that the spirit wars against the flesh, and the flesh against the spirit. The scene is now being set during the early teen years in a young person's life for this oncoming conflict which will have a far-reaching impact on their lives. Of course, the victorious young person is one who has suppressed and mastered these fleshly desires while allowing an ever increasing flow of spiritual and Biblical wisdom, truth, and application to have the preeminence in his or her life.

This is the time to draw near to your teen and become that friend with whom they can confide. Listen to and encourage their spiritual insights; don't correct errors they may make in their theology or application but rather help them expand the teaching if necessary. Through intimacy in these teen years, you will joyfully begin to see an ever increasing flow of spiritual wisdom in their lives. Have them check you on a few verses you have memorized or share with them a verse or two from which you have been lately encouraged. They will soon copy your example and begin feeding back the same to you. There is nothing more valuable than teaching your child how to draw counsel for their own lives from Scripture—this is the real basis for discipleship.

Most parents have been supplied through experiences of their own with enough knowledge drawn from their mistakes and success as a young person themselves to offer valuable guidance to their children. However, one thing that quickly turns a young person off to such counsel, as I mentioned before, is a legalistic parental attitude. A teen-ager no longer needs a lawgiver or school master but rather a friend in whom they can confide. Legalism, even if it is politely expressed, will tend to alienate your teen from you, and they will search for more accepting authorities or friends.

It seems ironic to me that in our society at the very age when a young person needs their parents' counsel and comfort the most, that somehow parents are convinced that now's the time for their teen-ager to get involved with a youth group or with others their same age who are facing similar struggles and temptations—and somehow together the young people will work out their problems. Just as parents have falsely reasoned that the school teacher is the most qualified person to teach their child academics, so also have they falsely reasoned that a youth leader can best meet their young person's spiritual needs—this really is not the best way.

Many of the temptations and lusts that Christian teens face are a product of following the social lifestyle of teen-agers in the world around them. One of the few specific directives for teens in the New Testament is the admonition to "flee" such involvements. "Flee also youthful lusts." II Tim. 2:22 The mid to late teen years should be the time when your teen begins to find his or her delight in seeking the Lord and meditating in God's Word. This is their best preparation for a successful future.

Seeking The Lord And Delighting In Him And His Word

As a child progresses into the teen years, keep on encouraging them to turn their hearts towards the Lord. We have consistently been blessed with a little woods in which my sons and I have been able to get alone for a walk and a time alone with the Lord. Encourage your young person to have a special time and place to meet with the Lord in prayer and meditation. Jesus often went by Himself into a lonely spot for a time of prayer.

Not long ago, one of my son's was expressing the joy he had experienced in one of these spiritual times he had with the Lord. He said emotionally, "Most people just don't understand how much joy the Lord can be." Once your children have experienced this kind of inner spiritual joy, they will recognize those things of the world that others learn to enjoy as only emptiness that will eventually let them down.

My daughters and my wife have similar spiritual times with the Lord in our home (which we have purposely gone to the expense and effort to make into a pleasant, worshipful, and spiritual environment.) They find rewarding spiritual times while playing the piano or organ and in singing Psalms, hymns, or spiritual songs. This brings them close to the Lord in spirit. Learning to delight ourselves in the Lord and His Word further builds our spiritual life while teaching us to be content with our present situation.

Waiting On The Lord

The Scriptures contain so many admonitions to wait patiently on the Lord, and this is another important aspect to teach our children—that the Christian walk requires the need to wait on the Lord for His provision of our needs in every aspect of life. For the older teen-ager, this waiting will fall into areas like finding a life partner or a ministry; and when the Lord and His Word have become their "delight" in this life, they will have much less difficulty waiting on these needs.

Remember, we live in a world in which most individuals have never recognized how God has supplied all of their needs. These same individuals often try to make parents feel guilty (and falsely so) if you are not encouraging your teen to be in social situations where they can find or choose a life partner. God works in miraculous and hidden ways to provide this need. Teaching our teens to wait and believe in God's goodness in providing in this area is extremely valuable for their Christian walk.

By thinking we are increasing our teen's "odds" for finding this partner through encouraging their social involvement really usually only makes waiting more difficult, encourages lust, emphasizes looking on the outward appearance, clouds their mind from seeing God's miraculous provision, and encourages them that one's needs can be provided aside from God's favor and supernatural ways. Ultimately, the faith of this teen is weakened through this human reasoning. Abraham and Sarah failed to wait on God for His miraculous provision for their life.

In Psalm 90:19, Moses wrote, "Establish thou the work of our hands upon us...." God's ministry for each of us in the body of Christ is, in itself, to be revealed to us in similar miraculous ways. It is sometimes difficult to wait on God to "establish the works" that He has for us in Christian service, but this is very much a need for our lives and our children's. It is so easy to substitute our human endeavors, efforts, or solutions to meeting this need in Christian ministry. Waiting on the Lord and seeing His guidance in this area is of great value to all our lives.

Time reveals the fruit of our faith and waiting.

As an example, when we first began to home school, our new, home-oriented lifestyle was looked down upon by many of our Christian acquaintances. One even said to me, "I don't know of ten Christian men in the whole country that believe the way you do." In those dawning years of home schooling, we honestly didn't know more than one or two families who were doing it either, but we stuck with it through many temptations and now rejoice to see literally tens of thousands of Christian men (and women) who believe the way we do. Waiting on the Lord for His ministry for our lives has with it many rewards. This is a most valuable truth to teach our young people.

Ruling The Spirit

Just as it is important to train our children to be sensitive to the promptings and leadings of the Holy Spirit in their lives, it is equally important to teach them to rule their spirit and emotions. Our emotions can swing to extremes such as excited happiness or depressed heaviness—neither of these states are really that desirable. One who cannot control his emotions or spirit is one who usually falls susceptible to good sounding teaching or teachers who offer little substance and truth for their actual life. "He that hath no rule over his own spirit is like a city that is broken down, and without walls." Prov. 25:28. He is like a defenseless city. Begin early to train your child to avoid emotional extremes in their life.

The word soberness in the New Testament conveys this idea of ruling of the spirit or emotions. In numerous places, young men and women are exhorted to be sober or sober-minded. (Titus 2:4 and 2:6, I Tim. 2:9, 2:15 and 3:11) I might note that by Jewish culture, a boy became a man around the age of twelve, so it is probably true that when Paul addresses young men or young women, he is likely talking to teen-age Christian young people.

This word sober has in it the concept of inner self-control which would include ruling one's emotions, passions, desires, etc. Now, of course, little children have a tendency towards silliness, laughing, giggling, etc.; this is part of being a child. But the time to start teaching your child to control this isn't when they have reached the age of twelve or thirteen—by this time the laughter has turned into a lack of self-control in various and different ways. When we observed our children's fun turning into an uncontrolled spirit of laughter or silliness, then we knew it had gone a little too far. Children can have fun without being excessively silly or foolish, but they also need help in controlling these temptations.

Occasionally, a child will have a tendency towards moodiness or melancholy (the opposite form of an unruled spirit). Regular intervals of encouragement and comfort from the parent will help this child gain a more level, emotional state. Sensitive parents who maintain an intimate level of communication with their children will detect their inner needs.

Parents and children alike begin to learn the value of ruling their spirits by building their direction and guidance in life upon Godly wisdom drawn from God's Word, rather than on our emotions. For example, if a group of women attempt to emotionally portray a lifestyle in which they are all excited about the way they are serving the Lord, yet on the other hand they are delegating the teaching and training of their children to others by sending them off to school, then wisely consider the probable outcome of this. Of course, God does use everything together for the good for those that love Him, but there are also consequences when priorities in Christian service are violated.

Caution your children about overly responding to others who try to appeal to them through flattery, being gushy, and other put-on forms of greeting. Both sons and daughters need to be discerning in this to avoid the allurement of those who would mislead them in various ways. This will help protect them morally. Children can learn to be friendly enough and kind without being captivated by these kinds of individuals.

There comes a time when our children should be outgoing, and this is when they have gained wise discernment to the temptations and foolishness in the world around them. If you encourage your child with these outgoing social atittudes before they are wise enough and strong enough to keep themselves from the world, you have done a great disservice to your child—not that we are attempting to keep our children from the world, but rather are preparing them so they are not *overcome* by the world.

"I pray not that thou shouldest take them out of the world, but that thou shouldest keep (protect) them from the evil." John 17:15 Just as people are expecting too much of children academically too early, similarly they are expecting too much of them too early socially.

Be cautious of those who try to make us think we want our children to learn to put on a smile or false happiness when this is not genuinely coming from within. There are many today who attempt to hide heaviness by such put-on emotions; eventually these outward shows or outward things we are doing will end, and then the real sorrow of heart will be overwhelming. "Even in laughter the heart is sorrowful; and the end of that mirth is heaviness." Prov. 14:13 It would be far better to teach our children the inner joy that comes from the Lord and obedience to His ways, the joy and peace that comes from being built up in the Lord daily.

Finally, purposely avoid music, speakers, or other situations that tend to make you or your children overly emotional. Emotionalism is often substituted for the emotions of inner joy and peace that Christ gives to us as we walk near to Him, delighting in Him in spirit.

The Meek Spirit

The lack of a meek spirit in one or more children (or the parents) in the family can disrupt the spiritual conditions in the home and cause stumbling blocks in training. The meek spirit has much to do with controlling conflicts and contentions of every sort, and for this reason, it is a quality much to be desired in the home.

The ultimate quality of beauty ascribed to the Christian wife in I Peter 3 is the "meek and quiet spirit." This is said to be of great value or price to God. There is no greater beauty that a mother can pass on to her daughter than the beauty of a meek and quiet spirit, and this will wonderfully prepare a daughter for her future marriage and life. Jesus described Himself in similar terms. He said, "For I am meek and lowly of heart." Matthew 11:29 So meekness is certainly a quality to be sought by fathers and husbands as well as wives and children.

In the Sermon on the Mount, Jesus said, "Blessed are the meek: for they shall inherit the earth." Matthew 5:5 Meekness, therefore, carries with it the expectation of inheriting the goodness of God in one's life upon the earth. Actually, meekness is the opposite of willfulness; it is thus one of the expected products found in the life of a child who has learned obedience.

Begin early teaching your child this quality. Help them learn to wait for someone to offer them a second glass of water or milk at meals instead of allowing them to ask for one. Meal times are one of the best times to be consistently teaching this quality; expect your child to eat what is set before them as much as is possible, and encourage them with quiet eating habits.

Try to meet your children's material needs like clothing or dolls and toys for little children within a reasonable length of time as the need arises. Be generous and giving within your means in this area. Your children will sense your giving spirit, and they will begin to model this in their own lives. When children have to wait a whole year (like for their birthdays) for basic needs or reasonable things that they would like, they tend to become lustful or greedy for such things.

Don't encourage them to ask for birthday gifts, but rather thoughtfully meet their needs by giving them something nice or even better than they would have expected. As they get older, they will be able to wait longer, and if the parents have been faithful in meeting needs in these younger years, the child will have an understanding that God gives good gifts in His perfect timing. "Every good gift and every perfect gift is from above." James 1:17 Providing good gifts for our children promotes meekness in their lives.

If you do celebrate Christmas, make it more of a Holy Day or holy time rather than an excessively materialistic time for children. A materialistic society tends to produce children with a lack of meekness towards life in general, and they tend to have greedy, willful children. So it is wise to discern proper influences in this area of gifts for your children.

Whining, complaining, or pulling on your arm while asking questions like, "When can we go, Mom?" are signs of lack of meekness. Of course, we need to be considerate of our child's frame; it is certainly difficult for them to wait patiently for several hours, but they should be able to wait quietly for an hour or so. As your child gets older, help them to recognize how God works through their parents (authorities) in different ways in their lives to meet needs and for guidance. The meek person is one who has learned to wait on God for their expectations and needs in life.

The Temptations Of Knowledge

One final area that we see as a potential disruption of the spiritual well-being of the home is this area of knowledge. Because of the vast availability of knowledge on virtually any subject today, there lies the danger of mental confusion and weariness due to excessive learning or knowledge. "And by these, my son, be admonished: of making many books there is no end; and much study is a weariness of the flesh." Ecclesiastes 12:12

Satan has had mankind on an endless trek for learning and knowledge from the beginning of creation, and has promised that knowledge would "open" their eyes to the answers of life. "...In the day ye eat thereof (the Tree of Knowledge of Good and Evil), then your eyes shall be opened..." Genesis 3:5b

Certainly coming to the knowledge of Jesus Christ as our personal Savior and growing in the truth and wisdom of Scripture will "open" our eyes to an abundant everlasting life. But Satan attempts to cloud man's mind to this life by offering the substitute of knowledge of any kind; and even after coming to Christ, many are made to stumble by the knowledge of good mixed with evil (the Tree of Knowledge of Good and Evil—Genesis 2:17).

One of Satan's greatest tools he uses to distract or confuse our minds to specific truth we may need for our lives is to throw all kinds of knowledge at us all day long—Bible knowledge as well as academic. It is like eating—we all need this for life, but we don't eat constantly. We allow time in-between for settling and digestion and to put to use the food we have eaten. This is the way Bible knowledge should be approached. It is different from academic study, although too much academics for a child who isn't quite ready for it can be discouraging for a child too.

We can actually find ourselves with a disorderly mind due to endless learning, knowledge, or study. We can find ourselves "ever learning" but not able to come to the knowledge of the truth we actually need for our lives. II Tim. 3:7 We can find ourselves "being carried about by every wind of doctrine" or teaching, or carried about with diverse and "strange doctrines." Eph.4:14 and Heb. 13:9 And those who often tempt us with such knowledge usually try to make us feel we are going to miss out on some valuable teaching for our lives if we neglect to hear or attend to their teachings.

Satan will tempt Christians with the knowledge of good mixed with evil so that we inadvertently pick up some evil that has been subtly and often inadvertently mixed in with some good—this is the Tree of the Knowledge of Good and Evil, of which we were told not to eat.

To avoid falling into this snare, place more emphasis on *doing* Scripture rather than hearing it. It is relatively easy to learn with our minds a certain Biblical truth, but it is yet another thing to be consistently living this on a daily basis—this takes grace. But once we are living it, we then are more fully understanding it and thus more able to convey this truth to others by our words coupled with the example of our lives. This approach to the Word along with deliberate resistance to the allurement of knowledge will protect and enhance our spiritual life. God knows how to guide us to the truth we need for our lives. Simply ask Him to do so.

And in the area of academics, it would be better to spend a good portion of the day working on manual skills, trade skills, or other more work-oriented activities that involve applied knowledge rather than on endless and exhaustive studies. It is helpful that curriculum suppliers have made available a wide range of materials

Further Spiritual Training

for the home schooling parent to select from, but try to limit your study load. Too much book work alone will not only wear out your child, but it may also cause burnout.

Wives and daughters are often more easily tempted with knowledge than boys or men are, although this is an area where we are all tempted to some degree. Remember, it was Satan who tempted Eve (not Adam) with the Tree of Knowledge of Good and Evil. We do need the knowledge of God's ways and truth for our lives. "My people are destroyed for lack of knowledge." Hosea 4:6 We all know we need knowledge, and for this reason Satan often tempts women in some way in this area.

In the past when I would bring home a newspaper or Christian book or magazine and would lay it on the counter top, my wife and two girls were usually attracted to them (although in recent years they have learned to resist such temptations). My wife and older daughter would even be tempted to flip through a few pages, but when my boys walked by and saw the paper or books, etc., they rarely were attracted to the covers and hardly ever picked them up to read them. It is wise to begin teaching daughters at a young age of this subtle temptation in this area of knowledge and to learn to develop a resistance to such temptations.

15

CHARACTER AND SOCIAL LIFESTYLE

Solomon observed that it was often the little foxes that spoiled the tender grapes. "Take us the foxes, the little foxes, that spoil the vines: for our vines have tender grapes." Song of Solomon 2:15 The garden is rarely under the threat of a sweeping plague or a devastating drought; but my, how often do they suffer from the intrusion of some furry little varment that soon robs us of the fruit of our labors.

The same is true in child rearing. So often in keeping our guard up against the formidable foes of the N.E.A. or misinformed legislators, we fail to recognize how yielding to those subtle and seemingly insignificant, social practices of the world around us can creep in and spoil our tender grapes. We are so easily persuaded to think we have an obligation to make our children like the world around them by little statements like, "Yes, but how will your children perform socially?" as if we were expected to train our children to live by the world's standards or act like children or young people of the world. It is time for Christian parents and children alike to realize we are supposed to be peculiar, odd, or different from the world around us.

Paul urged the Corinthian believers (believers who had adopted some of their social practices near to those of the world around them) to "come out from among them, and be ye separate, saith the Lord, and touch not the unclean thing; and I will receive you." II Cor. 6:17 The term "unclean" was a commonly understood expression with the early church. Christians recognized it as referring to the practices of those ungodly nations surrounding the nation of Israel. Those practices were not only to be rejected, but they were to be utterly destroyed so that the very thought or mention of such practices would be erased from their minds. But, unfortunately, today many Christians are not only touching unclean things (things or practices that the world around us readily accepts), but they are wholeheartedly embracing them.

The methods of allurement are often subtle. For example, Christians claim to justify their TVs for news and so-called educational programs, but many worldly ways and shameful things are conveyed even through and in-between these programs; and the family is often tempted with much more than this by having a TV set around the home. Excessive participation in sports, worldly Christian music, theatrical entertainment, and dancing are becoming commonly acceptable practices. A Christian missionary family wouldn't think of joining in with the idolatrous ways of the pagan culture to whom they were sent to minister, but somehow the pagan practices around us in America are, for the most part, overlooked.

Home schoolers are the pioneers of a new, Christian, social description. Let us be bold to continue to stand firmly on these new convictions whether it be in the home, neighborhood, marketplace, or the church that has adopted some of its social practices dangerously close to those of the world. Social practices come across into our own homes through many avenues. Let me discuss a few of these areas which are significantly affecting the social training of our children.

Character

There is much discussion today on the topic of development of character in children, but actually the very process of child training determines much, if not most, of the attitudes and character of your child. For example, a child who is allowed to be disrespectful of parental authority will tend to display a similar attitude towards their marriage partner, employer, or governmental authorities when older. A child who is allowed to be irresponsible with their schoolwork, keeping an orderly room, or other household tasks and responsibilities will, likewise, display similar traits when older.

A child who is allowed to be manipulative with his or her parents or brothers and sisters will tend to be this way towards their spouse when married. Children who have not been conditioned to sacrifice some of their personal enjoyment to accommodate the plans of their family will find it difficult to give and adapt to their marriage partner or others. The child also acquires much of their character from the example and modeling of the parental team and brothers and sisters, and once again character is certainly and significantly a product of companionships and communications. So while there is some value in studying character qualities as an intellectual or academic subject, it is essential we realize that, by and large, our child's character will ultimately be mostly a product of their daily life and conduct.

Though our character has much to say in regards to the world's perception of us, our character cannot be separated from God's perception of us. Jesus "increased in wisdom and stature, and in favour with God and man." Luke 2:52 Similarly, we see this in the life of Samuel. "And the child Samuel grew on, and was in favour both with the Lord, and also with men." I Samuel 2:26

There is character development which can make us pleasing and amiable with men only, but this is neither that desirable or even that possible if we are at the same time going to please God. If we have come to the point in our life when most men are speaking well of us, something is probably wrong. "Woe unto you, when all men speak well of you!"(Jesus speaking in Luke 6:26)

Jesus pleased God and man, but He certainly didn't follow the religious or social views of His day. In religion He walked in the spirit of Biblical truth rather than the tradional teachings of His day, and we know of the conflicts that this caused for Him. Jesus made a statement which reflected His attitude towards the socio-religious practices of His time: "But whereunto shall I liken this generation? It is like unto children sitting in the markets, and calling unto their fellows, and saying, 'We have piped unto you, and ye have not danced; we have mourned unto you, and ye have not lamented'. " Matt. 11:16 and 17

Many Christian home schoolers all across our nation are rediscovering a new social way of life and the resultant character that comes with it. They are choosing to be different from the world and worldly Christians in such things as dress, hair style, language, attitudes, music, family-home orientation, brotherly love, Christian devotion and service, leisure activities, home industry, Bible teaching, spiritual training, and many other things. They are tired of reaping the consequence of having troubled teens and children that has come from "dancing to the world's and worldly Christians' piping." So character development must go hand in hand with social interaction and lifestyle.

Colossians 2:8 not only warns us of the dangers of philosophy but also that of following traditions of men. You will notice a subtle "pressure" to conform to the social standards or social traditions set up by those who have a self-righteous attitude towards their knowledge and lifestyle.

We once moved to a small, rural community where people had prided themselves for years in their local, public grade school. Attendance at their school had become their symbol of righteousness, and it was amazing how many of these people looked down their pious noses at us home schoolers who dared to question the goodness of their tradition. You will find this same subtle pressure with many church groups and church schools, but the underlying problem with most of these is that they are still breaking down the unity of the home by their socialization practices.

Churches are constantly arranging teaching which is supposedly family and marriage building (and this is helpful), but many times the actual church programing and social activities tend to be counter-productive in these areas. Sometimes we find ourselves also under social pressures from relatives and, oddly to say, occasionally from other home schoolers or home schooling groups. We must be constantly evaluating these social-religious pressures because these involvements may be spoiling the tender grapes of our child rearing efforts.

Becoming Alert To False Guilt

There is often an underlying pressure exerted upon parents to follow religious and social norms or tradition, and we sometimes experience this in the form of false guilt. I remember feeling falsely guilty in the mid-seventies when I began to challenge the Christian tradition of sending children to church schools or Christian schools. I recall saying to myself, "You either must be way off or self-righteous to question the righteousness and effectiveness of such Christian works." However, after a while, I realized that I didn't have a judgmental spirit towards these works but rather a discerning spirit where I was exploring the possibilities of a better way.

In the days when the Apostle Paul wrote and admonished Christians to "beware lest any man spoil (lead you captive) through philosophy and traditions," most parents were probably teaching their own children the better part of their educational needs. So we can be sure Paul recognized there were many other traditions and philosophies other than educational ones by which Christians could subtly fall prey.

There is often a fine line between discernment and judgment, and those who want us to follow them or their traditions will often unfairly label all discernment as judgment in an effort to make us feel falsely guilty or as if we have been unreasonable in our considerations. I see home schoolers, as a whole, as those who are willing to take the heat for having a discerning spirit. But let us wisely consider any involvement and be willing to experiment with and give some new ideas a try. As in home schooling, time often shows the fruit of spiritual conviction.

Building Character Through Experiences

Character, for the most part, is a product of our everyday

life, and those things which we allow each day will become the building blocks that will eventually shape the character of our children. Take your child's dress habits or the orderliness of their room. If we allow our child to be sloppy, irresponsible, or careless on a daily basis with these tasks, they will develop corresponding character traits. There are many valuable character qualities children learn through performing household responsibilities such as: dependability; a servant's spirit; completeness; elimination of confusion which promotes a peaceful, productive and worshipful environment; responsibility; cooperation; a giving spirit; and many others.

Home industry, as we have said, builds family unity, but it has the added dimension of also building character in children. One of the foremost character qualities that Jesus taught His disciples was the servant's heart and spirit. "He that is greatest among you shall be your servant." Matthew 23:11 In Colossians, Ephesians, and Peter, we are exhorted to build this servant's spirit through our relationship to our employer, learning to do all things "as unto the Lord."

Home industries, where children first learn to work with dad and mom can, in so many ways, build these servant character qualities; and in this way, your child begins to learn the necessary qualities for serving Christ. Being a faithful servant requires many valuable qualities such as: dependability, responsibility, punctuality, a giving spirit, adaptability, cheerfulness, willingness, cooperation, respect, and many others. Like orderliness, the servant's spirit is a foundational character building block from which many other valuable character traits spring. Home schooling and home industry promote both of these foundational qualities.

Wisdom And Character

Wisdom is very much a part of character—we cannot separate the two. Take a quality like loyalty. Unless we teach our children wise spiritual and Biblical discernment, they (or we) could find themselves (or ourselves) becoming loyal to wrong causes or individuals.

The same is true for determination. It is very possible to be determined in ways in which God isn't truly leading us. There have been church groups who were determined to build an impressive building only to be overly burdened with debt and forced to use compelling tactics to satisfy this debt. In a multitude of business (determination), dreams come true. See Ecclesiastes 5:3. So as our children grow in character they will also need to grow in Biblical wisdom and discernment. Character and wisdom must go hand in hand.

Understanding Burnout

Related to this quality of determination and the human efforts that are often associated with it is the problem of burnout. It is far more important for Christians to learn to discern Christ's strengthening for their lives in given situations than it is to be determined in one's own strength to accomplish something. When we go beyond what the Holy Spirit is leading and strengthening us to do, we are likely at some point to experience burnout. Stronger individuals will not experience this burnout as readily nor as soon as weaker ones, but every one of us eventually will experience it to some degree if we fail to recognize how we are pushing ourselves beyond God's leading and promptings and strengthening for our lives and homes.

Jesus said, "My yoke is easy, and my burden is light." Matthew 11:30 When we are laboring (yoked) together with Christ, there will be *some* burden for us (and for some Christians this burden will be greater than for others); however, when we are doing the work Christ has for us, our flesh may seem somewhat burdened, but our souls will have a peace and a sense of restful satisfaction that will offset or balance out this burden. When we push ourselves beyond Christ's will or engage in something that is not His will, everyone involved will feel they are under an excessive load or burden, and this eventually leads to burnout.

There are several things we can do to prevent and minimize the effects of burnout in our lives:

1. Approach as many decisions and issues in life together with your spouse "as heirs together of the grace of life." Husbands may find they will need to give honor (a form of yielding) to their wife's feelings about certain situations or things that may seem excessively burdensome to her—"giving honor unto the wife as unto the weaker vessel." See I Peter 3. God has ordained wives to be the gauge that determines what the family can successfully bear.

At the same time, wives may sometimes not recognize when they also are trying to do too much. God usually uses the husband's oversight to recognize when his wife or children are excessively burdened. Fathers need to get a good "feel" of the lifestyle and academic workload in which his wife and children are involved—curriculums may be excessive, too demanding or difficult, confusing, etc. Also certain involvements may be making life too busy, confusing, or stressful.

2. Begin to try to sense the *Lord's strengthening* for your lives together. "The Lord is the strength of my life." Psalm 27:1 It is easy today to become overly involved in things we think, or others try to make us think, we should be doing for the Lord. It is also easy to find ourselves under a program and fail to recognize how this program has taken the place of God's direction and ultimate guidance in our lives. There are some programs that try to make parents feel that their children are going to be spiritually deprived or academically deficient if they are not involved with them.

The real joy of home training is finding our own family as our unique first ministry for Christ. This is a ministry for husbands and wives together, and all programs and curriculum should be available subservient to this structure of authority. Some Christians are more independent-minded than others, and some beginning home schoolers may find a curriculum program and schedule to be helpful when first getting started. Many times, however, an experienced home schooling family can help a beginning family to avoid getting a bad taste of home schooling that sometimes results from too much programing and scheduling or from excessive materials.

3. Be alert to overly rigid scheduling of your work day or academic deadlines. These can become hard task masters, too. Generalized scheduling and objectives are better. For example: My children know that on week days, in general, after domestic duties, we work on academics in the morning and early afternoon and then have time for music, crafts, manual skills, and vocational interests later in the afternoon; and we have Bible time over dinner or before bed on some evenings. Rigid scheduling can take the place of Christ's leading and strengthening for our lives.

4. Check priorities. There are many in Christian circles who try to make us feel like we are lazy in the Lord's work if we are first concentrating on our families for a season. There is constant subtle pressure from every imaginable source attempting to get us to neglect or be distracted from this foundational work for Christ.

5. Finally, some employment puts fathers under more of a demanding schedule than others. A lesser paying work where one has more freedom or where he works out of the home (or where the father is more available) is many times more desirable. I urge fathers to take the "step of faith" that is usually necessary in starting and maintaining a family or home-operated or oriented work of some kind.

Social Lifestyle In Character Development

An area of our lives which certainly plays a part in our character development is our acquired social way of life. The Bible gives us a fairly good description of desirable social qualities, but, unfortunately, much of what is being taught in this area has been tainted by social practices picked up from the world around us.

My oldest son was recently telling me about a Christian broadcast out of the United States that was going to be translated and aired in another country. However, the Christian man from that country who was going to be doing the translating said that he would have to censor the broadcast to fit more closely to his culture. For example, he stated that he wouldn't be discussing dating because it wasn't a custom of his society. Neither would he mention women getting into the car and going off alone, because it wasn't commonly practiced there.

Have we ever stopped to reason that perhaps those social customs might be closer to Biblical ways than our own? For years we have been trying to justify a Christian lifestyle that is similar to that of modern America by interpreting Scripture to accommodate this lifestyle.

Dating

Take this issue of dating. Nowhere in the Bible do we see a description of a boy-girl relationship that could be compared to the modern American practice of dating where a young man and woman go off together alone regularly prior to marriage. Most boy-girl relationships were built in group social situations (where the parents were present) or in situations where families were together. Anytime there was a relationship, it was for the ultimate purpose of marriage, not as a form of social pleasure or entertainment inspiring so-called "innocent" passions. These situations which could excite such passions were to be avoided until the young adult was mature spiritually where Christ's will and provision for his or her life has come first.

For example, Isaac wasn't seeking a wife. He knew that God would supply all his needs, and his delight was in the Lord. The Scriptures describe the contentment Isaac had in the Lord, for on the evening he met his future bride, Rebekah, he had gone into the fields to meditate on the Lord. See Genesis 24:63. It is not that Isaac didn't have a need in this area for the comfort and companionship of a wife—"and she (Rebekah) became his wife; and he loved her: and Isaac was comforted after his mother's death" (Genesis 24:67)—but even though he had this need, he recognized the futility in working on his own to supply it. The story of Ruth and Boaz beautifully describes two faithful believers who patiently waited for God to provide this need for a life partner. Neither of the two were seeking a mate when God brought them together miraculously.

Proverbs 18:22 says, "Whoso findeth a wife findeth a good thing, and obtaineth favour of the Lord." This word favour has in it the idea of good will or favourable action from God. In other words, God works it out in His secret and miraculous way to bring together a husband and wife, and God will work out this encounter through His omniscient guidance and timing. Parents were often involved in helping their children discern proper life partners, but God, Himself, is the ultimate counselor in knowing the arrangements necessary for "the way of a man with a maid." Prov. 30:19

Not all Christians marry, but most of us do; so a great part of the child training experience should involve training our children in proper understanding and attitudes of Biblical marital ways. Daughters need continual teaching in such areas as: true Biblical submission, adapting her ways to her husband's, the meek and quiet spirit, homemaking skills, child training skills, etc. Sons need to be prepared and trained in such Biblically described ways as: the giving of themselves for the spiritual, emotional, material, and physical needs of his wife; the loving spirit; adequate work skills or employment to provide for his home; and the realization that child training is, above all, his responsibility, etc.

For a more complete discussion of marital roles and responsibilities for both husband and wife, we suggest reading *Becoming Heirs Together Of The Grace Of Life*—also available through Parable Publishing House.

Sports

There are certain positive qualities that can be derived from sports such as cooperation, consideration, and self-improvement; but there are also some negative qualities that sports can produce which we should be alert to such as aggression, competitiveness, self-glory, self-confidence, pride, idleness, fleshliness, poor use of one's time, sibling and marital rivalry and jealousy, etc.

There are many sports in which families can participate that can enhance family unity and enjoyment together while avoiding or minimizing negative character, but sports should be analyzed for their spiritual value just as one would a book, tape, church, etc. Does the sport encourage sibling rivalry or envy? Does it create an aggressive, conquering, or competitive spirit? Does it place emphasis on winning rather than on wanting to build someone else up? Does it draw husbands or sons away from home, or does it unduly separate the family in some way? Does it encourage an independent spirit in wives or daughters? Does it cause women to be in unladylike positions? Does the sport excite youthful lusts or other temptations? Does it require the wearing of immodest apparel?

There is the need for exercise, but family hikes or walks and low or non-competitive sports can meet some of these needs while allowing for a relaxed time of communication and reflection.

Careers And Personality Traits

It is sadly surprising how many Christian girls and women are becoming career minded today. But isn't this the same goal of the modern American high school and college girl? Are we not once again patterning our lifestyle after the world around us? Wasn't the anticipation of having one's own home and being a support to one's own husband the original career and ministry designed for Christian girls?

Christian girls and women are furthermore being tempted to portray personality characteristics of the modern American woman. Sometimes Christian teen-age girls are described as bubbling, vibrant, a "live wire," and other similar terms with the assumption that these are qualities we would like to see in our daughters. To me, this decribes a girl who has little "rule" over her spirit or emotions.

The Bible talks about daughters learning to become sober in spirit and mind with shamefacedness, which is the opposite of being bold or outgoing. See I Tim. 2:9. These are considered as positive personality traits for the Christian girl. Her apparel should also indicate a conservative, reserved spirit within. The meek and quiet spirit attributed to the virtuous wife, found in

I Peter 3:1-6, gives us a similar description. There is a real need to realign the lifestyle-personality traits we are desiring for our daughters to a more Biblical standard. My wife has often remarked in regards to our daughters that she is not raising "career" girls but Godly young women who desire to love and serve Christ with their lives.

The Quest For Greatness

Another characteristic being exalted recently in Christian circles for young men is emphasis on the quest for greatness. There is talk of making our sons "champions" or "dynamic" or into "powerful speakers," etc. And, here again, these are traits that Christians have acquired from the world around them.

In these last days as we approach the second coming of Christ, we are told society would begin to once again portray a social lifestyle similar to that found in the days of Noah. "But as the days of Noah were, so shall also the coming of the Son of Man be." Matthew 24:37

In the days of Noah shortly before the flood, there was this similar emphasis on greatness that we are seeing today, "...the same became mighty men, which were of old, men of renown." Genesis 6:4 They were all competing for the top; they wanted to be renowned, great, or famous. We should expect unbelievers to act this way, but the goal for Christianity should be just the opposite.

Today in Christianity, we are beginning to idolize Christian athletes, concert performers, and those that have reached the rank of doctor just like society in the world around us; but God is not a respecter of persons. See I Peter 1:17 and James 2:1 and 2:9.

Godly Forms of Entertainment

The American society has become a play and entertainment-oriented society (just as the Roman Empire was before its decline), and Christians in America are similarly becoming entertainment-minded. I remember hearing an outspoken young woman who was the head of a large youth group of a fundamental church proclaiming to her congregation her goals for leadership: "We're going to show the world that we can have just as much fun as they can!" She then began to enumerate her menu of worldly entertainment and group activities she was planning for the youth group. Is this the goal of our youth? This is part of the reason why Christian youth face nearly as many temptations and lusts as worldly people do.

Entertainment has become a substitute for industriousness and inner joy. Some children have trouble finding something useful to do because their parents have come to believe it is part of their role in parenting to keep their child entertained. A better approach would be for parents to help their child learn to be industrious and to find inner joy and delight in the Lord, in nature (His creation), and in the Word. It is difficult for anyone who has become play oriented to settle down to work or be creative in finding something useful to do. Play oriented children will still have this tendency when older.

Societies tend to become play oriented when they have been led to believe that these play times are the only times they really enjoy in life. In times past, people learned to enjoy their work as much as their play. In fact, rarely can we enjoy our relaxed times unless we have done a good job at our labor. "The sleep of a labouring man is sweet..." Ecclesiastes 5:12

For example, one evening we had a family over for dinner. Our then ten-year-old daughter asked their daughter if she wanted to help her do the dishes while they talked. Their daughter commented while the two of them began working together, "I hate to do dishes!"

My daughter thought for a moment and then replied with a smile, "Well, we might as well learn to enjoy it because we're going to be doing them for the rest of our lives!" A lot of the problem lies in the attitude we have about our work, the attitudes we pick up from the world around us, and the attitudes we *allow* our children to have.

I remember several years ago one summer day buying some

softball equipment for my boys because the world was pressuring me into thinking they were really missing out on a lot of fun in life. I kept trying to tell my sons how much fun it was playing ball (I had spent a lot of my free time engaged in sports when younger), but they weren't so excited about it. Being raised on sports is a lot like being raised on TV; if you haven't been raised that way, it doesn't seem very important in life.

Well, my then fourteen-year-old son hit the ball a few times over our backyard fence and then said to me halfheartedly, not wanting to be a spoil sport or hurt my feelings, "Yeah, Dad, this is a lot of fun....How about let's go and build a little more fence together now?" We had been working together on some board fence using a post hole auger on the back of our tractor, and from then on we'd laugh and say that fence building was our favorite sport.

Our children enjoy "family nights" each week which are our relaxed times of play and entertainment, but they have each learned how to use their "free" time in productive and meaningful ways. When our oldest son was fourteen, he bought himself a nice, young draft horse with money he had saved by working for me. With advice from an old, horse-farmer neighbor of ours, my son learned about harness, horse-drawn equipment, and how to "break" and drive the horse. He very much enjoyed the time he spent with this horse for a few years. It is part of our role as Christian parents in child training to help our children find industrious activities to enjoy while teaching them to have the right attitude about work and to avoid an excessively play oriented lifestyle.

Setting a New Social Standard

The Christian home school should be far more than an alternative means of education. It should encompass an entirely different social way of life in all aspects as we have described in this particular chapter and throughout the book. So the next time some skeptic asks how your home schooled child will perform socially, tell them it all depends on whose social standards you are using to evaluate them. If they are asking if your children will be acting like worldly kids, talking or looking like worldly kids, enjoying the things worldly kids do or worldly Christians do, then the answer gladly is, "They *hopefully* are not performing that well."

16

HOME SCHOOLING, A ROAD TO GREATER SUCCESS

The reader who has covered the pages of this book has obviously seen a description of a family way of life that is different from that which has been commonly followed. Those who have embarked upon home schooling and home training their own children have, through their actions, dared to challenge the traditional ways. Be assured, this will not go unheeded by those who are comfortable with allowing others, for one reason or another, to take their place in the training and teaching of their own children.

If they can, in some way, convince themselves and others that we home schoolers have not been successful, then they can thus ease their own consciences. So we must be careful that we do not allow *them* to determine or set the standards for judging success, for they will in some way attempt to make us look like we have failed. Bear in mind that many of these individuals are, in reality, institutionally-minded and oriented. They have allowed the organization to take their place in child rearing, and they will also assume that a successfully trained young person is one who is fitting into the conventional ways that are considered successful.

For example, if you wanted to appear responsible or success-minded when I was in high school, you had to be planning on going to college. My opportunity to be apprenticed by my father in dental technology was looked down upon as some kind of lesser approach to a career. It's ironic that after quitting college my second year and returning to work with my father in his dental lab (where I had already gained many skills through after school and summer employment) that within a few years, I had college grads even with Master's Degrees approaching me, requesting opportunities to apprentice in lab technology. Of course, they were the ones who considered themselves "successful" since they had graduated from college, while I (though their employer and instructor) was not supposedly as successful; and I carried with me the stigma of being a college dropout.

My wife faced the same subtle peer pressure in the area of a career when in high school. She always had to have some kind of career in mind to answer everybody, and, of course, few young girls wanted to face the belittlement of saying they just wanted to be a wife and mother and take care of their home.

When I became a Christian and my wife re-dedicated her life to the Lord, the same pressures came at us from a different angle. Now, in some circles, success was determined if a young person was planning on attending a Christian college or Bible school, or by joining the staff of some missionary organization. These were now some of the standards that indicated one's sincerity and dedication, and we were not considered in full time Christian service unless we did.

In other circles, success was measured by one's willingness to join a religious group or by following certain teachers. For my wife, her success was also measured by her involvements away from home. Was she teaching a Bible study or involved with other women's groups? Somehow, child rearing was not considered successful, Christian service. It is rare to find a Christian in organization-minded America that doesn't think you should join or be affiliated with some organization to be truly on the road to success. So we need to be careful once again that we are not pressured by worldly or Christian traditions into thinking our children must follow their preconceived ideas of what is successful.

As we survey the Scriptures, it is obvious that God alone worked in lives and arranged circumstances to bring about the success of various individuals. For example, Abraham wasn't successful because he learned how to make wise business decisions in a competitive world. Abraham gave Lot his choice, and, of course, Lot made the logical, smart choice. Anyone could see that his choice would lead to prosperity. See Genesis 13:8-12. But we recognize in Abraham a non-competitive, meek attitude about his life, and God was with him and greatly blessed him.

We see this similar characteristic in Isaac. He chose to move on rather than to strive with others over the wells his men had dug. However, God was with Isaac—"And the man (Isaac) waxed great, and went forward, and grew until he became very great." Genesis 26:13

God also brought about circumstances to train His people for future service as in the case with Joseph, Daniel, David, and others. Joseph gained the skills needed to administrate the nation of Egypt through the famine by first taking care of Potiphar's house and managing the prison into which he was cast. David developed "skillful hands" to guide the nation of Israel by first responsibly taking care of his father's flocks, and it was no coincidence that a bear and a lion fell prey upon David's sheep. God knew he would need some skill and experience in seeing His miraculous protection in such situations.

Although Daniel and his comrades excelled academically, it was actually Daniel's spiritual abilities (given to him miraculously from God and aside from any works of his own) which allowed for the preservation of their lives and also brought about Daniel's eventual advancement in the Babylonian kingdom.

God works to bring about opportunities and circumstances which will prepare our children for their future as well as lead to prosperity in our children's lives provided that our motivation for home schooling lies primarily upon our desire to raise Godly children who love and fear God and desire to please Him with their lives. The world has always had its ladders to success, and today they may be called corporate or collegiate; but God would much rather choose "...the foolish things of the world to confound the wise; and God hath chosen weak things of the world to confound the things which are mighty; And base (lowly) things of the world, and things which are despised, hath God chosen...that no flesh should glory in His presence." I Corinthians 1:27,28, and 29

When we come to grips with the fact that *God brings success,* then our lives revolve around Him and His Word, not *our* ambitions, goals, or achievements in life. When we make the choice to take our children out of the classroom, at the same time we should decide that our children are now "separated" unto the Lord. God will work in surprising ways to make their lives successful, and faithfully watch for the opportunities He will bring along.

The Works Of Our Hands

God does have a work or ministry for each of our lives. "For the son of man is as a man taking a journey, who left his house, and gave authority to his servants, *and to every man his work,* and commanded the porter to watch." Mark 13:34 Again in I Corinthians 3:8b, we read, "...and every man shall receive his own reward according to his own labour."

There are priorities in our service for the Lord, and our first work would be to establish our own homes and to have the confidence that this first work is settled before moving ahead to the next. Indeed, God will bring further work for us when He sees we have brought our first work to a place of stability and predictability.

It's like building a house. Often we want to get the walls up and the roof on so it looks like we are getting the job done or so that others can see all that we are doing. But if we hurry ahead and neglect to set first the foundation, all our glorious works above will in time crumble, bringing ridicule from those around.

Discipleship, Our Ultimate Goal

There can be no doubt that the ultimate goal that we as Christian parents have in child training and home schooling is to see our children grow into young adults walking with the Lord, desiring to serve and please Him. If we fail in this area, no amount of academic success, apprenticeship skill, or character development can offset this loss.

Discipleship is, for the most part, passed on to our children by example. For this reason, church involvement and seeing your home as a place of ministry and worship plays an important part in this area of discipling our children. Rarely a week will pass for us without an opportunity to minister as a family to those who come to our home. We have also in recent years had the opportunity to be involved with church groups made up, for the most part, of home schooling families where the fathers (who have led their own families well) have taken the teaching and leadership responsibilities in the church. We were surprised and thankful to observe that the teens in these churches almost in entirety were walking with Christ, having a desire to live and serve Him with their own lives, and we rarely saw any incidences where the children were straying from Christ.

The logical explanation for the higher degree of success in these kinds of church environments has to be that the young people are learning to follow the example set by their fathers and mothers as teachers and seeing their parents' willingness to be separate from the world while keeping their families together. Remember that, as the Apostle Peter states, the church leaders were to be "examples to the flock." The young men in the church tend to learn from the example of their fathers or other older men in the congregation the importance of gaining Biblical knowledge and application for those they will need to be responsible for in the future (first, their own wives and children, and then later, the congregation of believers).

"For if a man know not how to rule his own house, how shall he take care of the church of God?" I Timothy 3:5 Church leadership was perpetuated in the early church by this kind of tutorial/apprenticeship approach, and those of us who are in home schooling recognize the distinct advantages and superiority of these two teaching methods.

Furthermore, because many home schooling fathers are responsibly teaching Bible truth in their homes (they are "apt to teach") and are learning to "rule their own houses well" (I Tim. 3:4), they are many times very good examples to follow in the church and often just as knowledgeable of Biblical truth because they have been *living* and *applying* it at home. Other distinct advantages to this type of church involvement is that it allows for the passing on of church leadership, teaching, and ministry skills to our children without thinking these skills can only be learned at an institution.

We would encourage home schooling parents to find or to have in their own home a small cell group from their larger church or perhaps a fellowship type church which allows for more interaction and edifying of one another, and where children can see their fathers actively exhorting and counseling others in Biblical ways on a regular basis. It would also be good for daughters to see their mothers in this setting encouraging other Christian wives in ways which direct other women to their own homes. "That the aged women...may teach the young women to be sober, to love their husbands, to love their children, to be discreet, chaste, keepers at home, good, obedient to their own husbands, that the Word of God be not blasphemed." Titus 2:3-5

Conclusion

We do recognize there are no perfect church methods any more than there is a perfect home school, or, better yet, a perfect Christian; but those of us in home schooling have come to realize that there *is* a better way to educate our children. In Philippians, Chapter 1, verse 10, we are urged to approve things that are excellent (better or best), and those in home schooling are discovering a *better* way to have a more predictable and sure outcome in the training of their children. We are not claiming to have reached perfection, but we are seeing greater success.

It has been our hope that, through the pages of this book, you have discovered some *better* ways or ideas for the training of your children. Perhaps a few of these ideas may have been somewhat new to your thinking, but we would like to encourage you to thoughtfully and prayerfully consider these concepts and allow God the time to validate them as wholesome and productive for the creation and maintenance of the Godly Christian home—to the glory of God. *"Consider what I say; And the Lord give thee understanding in all things."* II Timothy 2:7

ADDENDUM

Spanking in Today's Society

by Dr. James Sherman, Christian Pediatrician and
Home Schooling Father

Governmental intrusion into every aspect of our lives is becoming more and more a problem. In no other area is this as potentially frightening as in the area of spanking. Because of the seriousness of child abuse, social service agencies have been given great powers to intervene in order to protect children. Health care workers are by law *required* to report cases of *possible* child abuse or risk losing their licenses. Upon receiving a report, a social worker is required to investigate and can easily obtain a court order to remove a child from a home.

Most social workers have been taught that all forms of "corporal punishment" (including spanking) are wrong, and many of their organizations are actually encouraging laws to prohibit all forms of "corporal punishment." This ungodly influence is slowly changing societies' attitude toward spanking. Spanking is now illegal in Sweden. There are many instances of children being removed from Godly homes. Although, in most cases, the children are eventually returned, the emotional and financial costs to a family can be very large. In order to protect yourself and your family, the following are suggested:

a. Ask your pediatrician or family doctor if they suggest spanking as a form of discipline. If they do not, find another doctor. Many medical societies now have position statements against "corporal punishment", but most communities will have a Christian physician who will support you. Discuss the issue thoroughly with the physician. This can be an important protection should you be unfortunate enough to end up in court.

b. Spanking should be done in privacy both to protect yourself from charges of abuse and your child from the embarrassment of public humiliation. If you are in a public place, usually taking the child to your car will provide adequate privacy. Be careful in other people's homes. Child abuse charges have arisen from "friends" and even close relatives.

c. Physical evidence is considered highly suggestive of excessive force. If your spanking leaves bruises, consider changing the method you use. A "reed-like" rod will produce a sting but less bruising than a heavy stick.

d. Be discrete if the spanking has inadvertently caused a bruise.

Spanking done by an angry, out of control parent may, indeed, be abusive. Done by a loving parent in a controlled manner, spanking is God's best answer to the problem of disciplining our children.

FOOTNOTES

[1] Gregg Harris, *The Christian Home School*, (Brentwood, TN: Wolgemuth & Hyatt, Publisher, Inc., 1988), p. 54.

[2] Raymond and Dorothy Moore, *Home Grown Kids*, (Waco, TX: Word Books Publishers, 1981), p. 122.

[3] Raymond and Dorothy Moore, *Home-spun Schools*, (Waco, TX: Word Books Publishers, 1983), p. 21.

[4] Connecticut Blue Laws of 1650 from *The Annals of America*, (Encyclopaedia Britannica, 1976), Vol. 1, p. 201.

[5] Bill Gothard, *Advanced Training Institute of America Newsletter*, (Oak Brook, IL: Institute in Basic Youth Conflicts, 1989), Vol. 1, p. 1.

[6] John W. Whitehead and Wendell R. Bird, *Home Education and Constitutional Liberties*, (Westchester, IL: Crossway Books, 1984), p. 22.

[7] Gregg Harris, *The Christian Home School*, (Brentwood, TN: Wolgemuth & Hyatt, Publisher, Inc., 1988).

[8] J. Richard Fugate, *What the Bible Says About...Child Training*, (Tempe, AZ: Aletheia Division of Alpha Omega Publications, 1980).

[9] Al and Pat Fabrizio, *Under Loving Command*, (Palo Alto, CA: Sheva Press, 1989), pp. 20-22.

[10] Andy Barth, *Peace I Give Unto You*, (Charlotte, VT: Parable Publishing House, 1990).

[11] Jeff Barth, *A Thanksgiving Story in Vermont—1852*, (Charlotte, VT: Parable Publishing House, 1989).

[12] Jeff Barth, *Papa Leonardo*, (Crockett, KY: Rod and Staff Publishers, 1988).

[13] Elsie E. Egermeier, *Egermeier's Bible Story Book*, (Anderson, IN: The Warner Press, 1969).

NOTES

NOTES